IN *His* FOOTSTEPS

To Martha,

"Lord, I am coming!"
                    Ps. 27:8 NLT

Jayne Rogers Foster
♡

GAYLE ROGERS FOSTER

IN *His* FOOTSTEPS

A 90-DAY DEVOTIONAL TO ENJOY *Jesus* DAILY

Featuring Daily Words of Wisdom from
ADRIAN ROGERS

Copyright © 2025 by Gayle Rogers Foster
All rights reserved.
Printed in the United States of America

979-8-3845-1565-4

Published by B&H Publishing Group
Brentwood, Tennessee

Dewey Decimal Classification: 242.64
Subject Heading: DEVOTIONAL LITERATURE /
BIBLE—INSPIRATION / BIBLE—READING

Unless otherwise indicated, all Scripture references are taken from the *Discover God Study Bible*, New Living Translation, copyright © 1996, 2004. Used by permission of Tyndale House Publishers, Inc., Carol Stream, Illinois 60188. All rights reserved.

Scripture references marked AMP are taken from the Amplified Bible, copyright © 2015 by The Lockman Foundation, La Habra, CA 90631. All rights reserved.

Scripture references marked ESV are taken from the English Standard Version. ESV® Text Edition: 2016. Copyright © 2001 by Crossway Bibles, a publishing ministry of Good News Publishers.

Scripture references marked KJV are taken from the King James Version, public domain.

Scripture references marked NASB are taken from the New American Standard Bible®, Copyright © 1960, 1971, 1977, 1995, 2020 by The Lockman Foundation. All rights reserved.

Scripture references marked NIV are taken from the New International Version®, NIV® Copyright ©1973, 1978, 1984, 2011 by Biblica, Inc.® Used by permission. All rights reserved worldwide.

Scripture references marked CEV are taken from the Contemporary English Version, copyright © 1995 by American Bible Society For more information about CEV, visit www.bibles.com and www.cev.bible.

Scripture references marked NKJV are taken from the New King James Version®. Copyright © 1982 by Thomas Nelson. Used by permission. All rights reserved.

Cover design by Jonathan Lewis, Jonlin Creative Design. Cover images by Mywalkmindway/Shutterstock and kiwihug/unsplash.

All Adrian Rogers' quotes at the end of each devotional were taken from his notebooks that his daughter now has.

1 2 3 4 5 6 • 28 27 26 25

Contents

A Note from the Author	1
Day 1: Hide It in Your Heart	5
Day 2: Seeing from God's Perspective	7
Day 3: True Servanthood	9
Day 4: Should You Really Make These Three Proclamations Every Day?	11
Day 5: Waiting on the Wind	13
Day 6: A River in the Rock	15
Day 7: Turning the Table on the Devil	17
Day 8: Into the Unknown	19
Day 9: Are You Stressed over Money?	21
Day 10: Open My Eyes, Lord	23
Day 11: All Relationships Are Not Created Equal	25
Day 12: Other People's Needs	27
Day 13: What Has God Already Told You to Do?	29
Day 14: It's All in How You Say It	31
Day 15: God's Gift Closet	33
Day 16: Run for Your Life	35
Day 17: A Grace Vending Machine	37
Day 18: Are You Qualified?	39
Day 19: Vive la Différence	41

Day 20: The Right Goal	43
Day 21: Even Though	45
Day 22: The Whole Truth and Nothing but the Truth	47
Day 23: You Can Learn to Speak a New Language	49
Day 24: Because You Are United in Christ	51
Day 25: The Lion King	53
Day 26: But It's So Hard!	55
Day 27: You Might Be the Cause of Your Own Problems	57
Day 28: Ministry or Manipulation?	59
Day 29: Check-Ins for Schedule Review	61
Day 30: Are Successful People Successful?	63
Day 31: Building on the Right Foundation	65
Day 32: How Do you Choose?	67
Day 33: Pain Precedes New Birth	69
Day 34: No First Amendment Rights with God	71
Day 35: Sometimes You Just Need to Climb a Tree	73
Day 36: It Won't Cost Anything but Time	75
Day 37: Your Emotional Warning Light Is On	77
Day 38: The Top Five Things You Need to Do Every Day	79
Day 39: Are You on the Verge of Giving Up?	81
Day 40: You Are the GOAT at Being You	83
Day 41: Complete in Christ	85
Day 42: Is God Enough?	87
Day 43: Tears in a Bottle and Hairs on Your Head	89
Day 44: True Love	91
Day 45: How to Become Obedient	93
Day 46: A Lost Phone	95
Day 47: It Is Time!	97

Day 48: How to Love People You Don't Like	99
Day 49: What If God Is Giving You a Second Chance?	101
Day 50: Standing at the Crossroads	103
Day 51: Dying with Grace because of Dying Grace	105
Day 52: Are You Waiting on God, or Is God Waiting on You?	107
Day 53: Drinks Are on the House!	109
Day 54: Relational Stewardship	111
Day 55: Helping Others Finish Well	113
Day 56: I Have a Hunch He Wants Your Lunch	115
Day 57: Is Your Mind Out of Alignment?	117
Day 58: Become a Stronger Leader	119
Day 59: Open Doors and Closed Doors	121
Day 60: Humility Is the Key	123
Day 61: It's Already in Your Closet	125
Day 62: Character Qualities That Will Increase Your Influence	127
Day 63: If You Are Sold, You Will Be Bold	129
Day 64: Is Your Elevator Going Up or Down?	131
Day 65: When Submission Is Difficult to Understand	133
Day 66: He Knows Your Name	135
Day 67: What Happens When You Submit to Someone Who Is Undeserving?	137
Day 68: Do What You Said You Would Do	139
Day 69: Making a Connection	141
Day 70: Be a Praise Detective	143
Day 71: One Size Fits All	145
Day 72: Quit Serving God Leftovers	147
Day 73: The Hopelessness of Shame	149
Day 74: My Mother Could Eat All the Jelly She Wanted	151

Day 75: Do the Work	153
Day 76: Finding Happiness	155
Day 77: Break a Leg	157
Day 78: Entrepreneurs for Jesus	159
Day 79: I Am Learning to Love the Wind	161
Day 80: The Deception of Self-Protection	163
Day 81: But First, Clean Your Room	165
Day 82: Memorize It, Utilize It, and Weaponize It	167
Day 83: God Himself Is Your Armor	169
Day 84: Walking in the Fire with Jesus	171
Day 85: A Little Thing Is a Big Deal	173
Day 86: God Will Give You More Than You Can Handle	175
Day 87: Small but Mighty	177
Day 88: The Lost Art of the Handwritten Note	179
Day 89: Are You Emotionally Needy?	181
Day 90: Let God Work the Night Shift	183
Notes	185
Personal Reflection	187

A Note from the Author

I am not a brilliant scholar or a widely known speaker. What I have to say primarily comes from time spent sitting at the feet of my Father, not time spent through academic pursuits. My father is, indeed, Adrian Rogers, arguably one of the most influential ministers in the last century. You will experience his fingerprints that have molded my heart in every devotional and specifically in the quote or "Adrianism," as they are lovingly referred to, at the end of each day. I would not be who I am today without his influence. He was anointed and sold out to Jesus like none other.

In the fourth quarter of my life, I have sat on the bench next to his grave site and pledged to take his baton and pleaded for his mantel. I have walked step-by-step over every inch of sod covering his body and claimed every prayer he ever prayed for me. The first three-quarters of my life were spent trying to make certain no one discovered who my father was, yet the final quarter has been spent shouting it from the rooftops. This book is dedicated to him. He is my hero and maybe yours too.

Adrian Rogers, however, is not the father I am speaking about when I refer to time spent sitting at the feet of *my Father*. The father I am speaking of is my *heavenly Father*. In my time with Him, I have finally learned the blessing of brokenness and the secret of surrender. I have learned that when I empty myself of me and sit at His feet, He will fill me with Himself.

These devotional thoughts are what my heavenly Father has poured into my broken, empty vessel so that I can take them and pour them into yours. These words have come from waiting, not from working. They have come through abiding, not through accomplishments. I am nothing more than a carrier and a conduit of His grace.

This book is dedicated to my earthly father, Adrian Rogers, but is written to give glory and honor to my heavenly Father. I pray you will sense that. I pray you will open your own heart to receive it.

This book is also dedicated to my mother, Joyce Rogers. If I am in the final quarter of my life, my mother is certainly in overtime. While some grow weary and bitter as they age, my mother has become kinder than she already was and even more grateful. There are a few things mother doesn't remember. She doesn't remember offenses. She can't remember anything about me that grieved her while I was growing up. Truthfully, she can't remember, or chooses not to remember, any offenses against her. What she doesn't remember sometimes amazes me. What she does remember is what amazes me the most. I would love to forget what she has forgotten and remember what she remembers.

Mother always remembers that she loves Jesus and that He loves her. She remembers Scriptures that are tucked so deeply into her heart that the cruel limitations of age have been unable to take them from her. My eyes fill with tears as I think about the things she *does* remember. She always remembers to ask about me and pray for me—right on the spot and immediately. The less she is able to do physically, the happier she has become to simply sit in His presence. I would have thought it would frustrate her. It doesn't. She is content with Jesus. Her body isn't quick like it used to be. Her mind is slowing down. But it is slowing down to the pace of being able to savor everything her Savior has done for her. May I have a mind that thinks at that pace. So many times my mind races right past where God wanted it to pause. Mother, I love you! Even at my age, I still want to be like you when I grow up.

To my beloved husband, Mike. It brings such joy to my heart to see you serving and using the gifts God has placed within you. I cherish your wisdom, I rest in your protection, I am so grateful for your love.

Where would I be without you and the beautiful family you have given to me? Michael, Caty, Becket, Pia, Clement, and Therese—I love living next door to all of you and watching you grow up loving Jesus. Adrian and Kimberley—you amaze me with your gifts, talents, and kindness. I love *all* of you. I love *each* of you.

I cannot thank everyone, but there are a few special people who were instrumental in making this particular book happen: Donna Gaines, I think you and my father are just about two of the best Bible teachers I have ever heard! I am indeed blessed to have sat under both of you. This book would not have happened without your influence. I'm not certain whether I love what is inside of you the most or what radiates outside of you. Both are pretty incredible!

Thank you to my dear friend, Rhonda. Proverbs 27:9 says, "The heartfelt counsel of a friend is as sweet as perfume and incense." So many of you have ministered to me and prayed for me. Rhonda has especially been with me in the trenches during this project. There are so many others. Elizabeth, you have such wisdom. Raenell, you not only speak God's Word to me, but you always speak a word from God *into* me—which is just another level. Susan, you have helped in so many practical ways. Susie, your prayers have reached heaven. Pat, your vision for me is coming true. Donna L., who wouldn't want you in their court? My women's Bible study small group, my Sunday morning life group, my Wednesday night dinner friends—I have been enriched by each of you. I cherish the extended family support from both the Rogers family and the Foster family. There isn't a single one of you that I don't love. I love my Premier family. I won't ever forget you. And last but not least, who said you can't love your Facebook friends? I love you like you are sitting in the chair next to me every day.

I look forward to sharing with each of you what God has poured into me. I *really* look forward to learning that this book has inspired you to hear from God yourself. He wants to use my words to minister to your heart. He gave them to me for you, but He really wants to give you words of your own. Meet Him in *your* secret place. He is waiting to talk to you. He has something He wants to say. Begin to write *your own* devotionals in *your* personal journals!

Day 1

Hide It in Your Heart

I have hidden Your word in my heart, that I might not sin against You. . . . I have recited aloud all the regulations You have given us.
Psalm 119:11, 13

As you read these daily devotions, I invite you to join with me in making Scripture your own through memorization and meditation. As I am writing this, my goal for this year is to memorize part or all of the book of Ephesians. I desire for this particular book to become part of my default thinking pattern. Ask the Holy Spirit to put a chapter or an entire book of the Bible on your heart. There is something unique that He wants to say to you, and He knows exactly where it is found in His Word. He will lead you to what you need to memorize and make your own. Pick a translation that is easy for you to understand and get started today. If you don't know what to do, then join with me in the book of Ephesians. Here are some practical tips:

Type and print out your selected passage. Cut it and tape it on a note card (about three verses at a time). Take this note card with you everywhere you go. You wouldn't go without your phone; don't go without your Scripture card! Pull it out and read it as often as you would check your texts or your Facebook feed. Stay with one card until you are able to quote it word for word. Roll the rich meaning of each phrase around and around in your mind. Place your emphasis on a different word each time you repeat the verse. That adds layers of meaning. Apply the truth of these verses to everything you do in the course of your day. If you long for God to speak to you, just speak the words you are memorizing out loud.

Meditate on your verses the last thing before you fall off to sleep. You won't believe what God will plant in your mind while you are sleeping. Turn the phrases into prayer back to God. Claim the promises. Change your behavior because of them. Before you move on to another few verses, make certain you pass the truths you have learned to the people God will sovereignly put in your path, whether they are family members or strangers. God puts it into you, in order for it to flow out of you. It is from God, to you, and then through you.

"I don't care what is in your mind. God can renew your mind. God can cleanse your mind."
Adrian Rogers

Day 2

Seeing from God's Perspective

*"But forget all that—it is nothing compared to what I
am going to do. For I am about to do something new.
See, I have already begun! Do you not see it?"*
Isaiah 43:18–19

Circumstances look vastly different from heaven's perspective. We are unable to see God's purpose in the plan because all we can see is our pain in the present. We can't see what is coming next. Many times, losing things can actually be progress. A few years ago, we had a forty-year-old pine tree that needed to go. The falling limbs were dangerous. The grass couldn't grow because this tree was blocking the sun. The tree had taken over, but I didn't want to pay the money required to have it removed. What I couldn't see from my perspective was that the giant tree was occupying a space that would hold a play fort for my grandchildren, who in the future would be moving right next door. I couldn't see that the grass needed to grow where those tiny precious bare feet would run. All I knew was that even though I was told it was dangerous, I was accustomed to it and certainly didn't want to spend the money to have it cut down. Though the situation wasn't perfect, it was good enough for me.

How often does good enough keep us from best? Rest assured, if God is taking things away, it is for your good. He is creating a space for something better. Strongholds have to go. Idols need to be torn down.

Learn to rejoice in necessary endings. They are good, not bad. The things that are falling in your life might actually be falling into place.

A few years back an "expert" in the stock market said this market wasn't going to turn around until the S&P dropped another 10 percent. He said another 10 percent down was the point where he would load up. There are so many spiritual analogies. Going down is oftentimes the path to going up. When you humble yourself, you will be exalted. When you clear space, new growth can begin. When something old ends, something new starts. Necessary endings lead to more exciting beginnings.

"Don't ask God to cram His plan into your puny little mind because then God would be limited by your understanding."
Adrian Rogers

Day 3

True Servanthood

*And since I, your Lord and Teacher, have washed your
feet, you ought to wash each other's feet. I have given you
an example to follow. Do as I have done to you.*
John 13:14–15

Are you really a servant? Or do you just periodically do nice things? What is your motive when you do those nice things? Do you want praise or possibly to feel warm and fuzzy on the inside? Many times people do what some might call "serving" simply to ingratiate the recipient. Your "community service" might be nothing more than good PR. Someone has wisely said, "If you want to see if you are really a servant, see how you act when someone treats you like one."

There are two qualities of servanthood that I think separate servanthood from mere politeness.

First, a true servant doesn't just do things for others when it is easy. It's okay to do the easy things. You ought to. It is nice to hold doors open for others and help someone carry something heavy. Doing things like this is a part of being a decent human being. But a true servant inconveniences herself for the needs of others. She does things that actually cost her something in time, effort, or money. She goes out of the way. She gets dirty. She misses out on something else she would have liked to have done because she was serving others.

Second, a true servant doesn't do things in order to build up goodwill in a bank account from which she can make withdrawals when needed. That could be more manipulation than ministry. A true servant serves others who can never do anything for her in return. Many times true servanthood is anonymous. Your repayment should be from God, not the person you served.

> *"The world judges a person by how many servants he has. Jesus measures us by how many people we serve."*
> **Adrian Rogers**

Day 4

Should You Really Make These Three Proclamations Every Day?

*He must become greater and greater,
and I must become less and less.*
John 3:30

I read a women's health magazine in the doctor's office that said you should make these three proclamations every day: "I am strong." "I am beautiful." "I am enough." Truth or error? It depends! Let's dig into it and see what God's Word says.

"**I am strong.**" Actually, thinking I am strong is what gets me into trouble. God's Word says when I am weak, *then* I am strong because I am forced to depend on His strength: "'My power works best in weakness.' So now I am glad to boast about my weaknesses, so that the power of Christ can work through me. That's why I take pleasure in my weaknesses, and in the insults, hardships, persecutions, and troubles that I suffer for Christ. For when I am weak, then I am strong" (2 Cor. 12:9b–10).

"**I am beautiful.**" The only thing beautiful about me is the Jesus inside me. "We are all infected and impure with sin. When we display our righteous deeds, they are nothing but filthy rags" (Isa. 64:6). There is nothing I can brag about apart from Him. I am beautiful. But what is beautiful is only what He has done.

"**I am enough.**" God's Word clearly says that I am woefully inadequate: "For everyone has sinned; we all fall short of God's glorious standard" (Rom. 3:23). I am only enough when I am complete in Him: "So you also are complete through your union with Christ" (Col. 2:10a).

So go ahead and make those proclamations. You are strong! You are beautiful! You are enough! But only make them in the truth of who you are *in Christ*. Positive thinking and positive proclamations apart from those two little words "in Christ," are dangerous. Don't fall for humanism masked in "positive speak." But never hesitate to claim the real truth: "For I can do everything through Christ, who gives me strength" (Phil. 4:13).

*"I wouldn't trust the best fifteen minutes
I ever lived to get me into heaven."*
Adrian Rogers

Day 5

Waiting on the Wind

*He released the east wind in the heavens and guided
the south wind by His mighty power.*
Psalm 78:26

I read a book recently that profoundly impacted the way I think about the will of God. The book was *Opportunity Leadership* by Roger Parrott. In that book, he contrasts sailboats with powerboats. A powerboat sets its sights on the goal and powers through the obstacles. It decides in advance where it is going, turns on the engine, and motors through. A sailboat, on the other hand, waits for the wind to fill its sails and only goes wherever the wind might lead. These are two different types of boats, and they represent two different types of people.

For the majority of my life, I have been that powerboat. I have falsely believed I was following God, when in fact, I was providing my own power. What I thought of as following God was far more asking God to follow me. I built my life on the twin towers of proactivity and strategy. My motto was: "Plan your work and work your plan." I thought I was pleasing to God. In reality, I was attempting to live the Christian life by common sense, instinct, intellect, and willpower.

I have never liked to wait. I have always held proactivity to be one of the highest virtues. I lived the quote, "Just do something, even if it's wrong." I convinced myself that people who waited were procrastinators. And in addition to being lazy, procrastinators missed opportunities. I remember a business training where I boldly said, "Most of you who say you are waiting on God, aren't waiting on God at all. You are just waiting." What I would give to go back and do that training again. It would be a different training.

I now realize that God doesn't need me or even want me to be a powerboat. He wants me to be a sailboat. He wants me to wait on His wind. But He *does* want me to wait with my sails up. When He is ready to move, He will provide the power. He will provide the direction. And He can change that direction at any time He desires. His will may be found in what I would have assumed was a detour or a setback. The wind comes from Him, not from me.

I want you to learn that when it is completely still, you just need to wait. Wait and listen. Wait and watch. Be still, but ready. As you wait, be completely tuned into the gentlest breeze and the slightest change in direction. Do not set your own goals and provide your own power. Set your sails and be completely surrendered to the breath of the Holy Spirit.

"We set the sail; God makes the wind."
Adrian Rogers

Day 6

A River in the Rock

*He split open rocks in the wilderness to give them water,
as from a gushing spring. He made streams pour from the
rock, making the waters flow down like a river!*
Psalm 78:15–16

Nothing sounds less appealing than rocks in the wilderness. And conversely, nothing sounds more appealing than gushing springs and streams flowing down like a river. One is a barren nightmare, the other a lush paradise. And yet, amazingly, the two are found in the same place.

The book of Exodus says that the children of Israel were wandering. They were tired. They were thirsty. They angrily demanded water, and instead of thanking Moses for leading them out of bondage, they argued with him saying, "Why did you bring us out of Egypt? Are you trying to kill us, our children, and our livestock with thirst?" (Exod. 17:3b).

Though God had miraculously delivered them on dry ground through the sea, they soon forgot. How could they possibly have forgotten that? But you and I are guilty of the same thing. In the middle of today's mess, we can't remember yesterday's miracle. We are appalled at the children of Israel while doing the same thing ourselves. We excuse ourselves by saying they were eyewitnesses. Yet we have access to the entire Bible. We are living after the incarnation, crucifixion, and resurrection. We have the Holy Spirit inside of us. We are without excuse!

We, too, forget the miracles and focus on the rocks. What we fail to see through the eyes of faith is that the rocks in our wilderness represent Christ. First Corinthians 10:4 says, "And all of them drank the same spiritual water. For they drank from the spiritual rock that traveled with them, and that rock was Christ." They were complaining that God had forsaken them when the New Testament tells us Christ was the spiritual rock that traveled with them. They looked at the stones and never saw the Savior.

How do you find the Redeemer in the rocks? How do you experience the Savior in the stones? There is only one way. It is through brokenness. When Moses was told to strike the stone, it was a foreshadowing of Jesus, who was smitten for our sins. Because His body was broken for us, He could say, "Anyone who is thirsty may come to Me! Anyone who believes in Me may come and drink! For the Scriptures declare, 'Rivers of living water will flow from his heart'" (John 7:37b–38). This water came because Jesus was broken for you, and your thirst will only be quenched when you are broken for Him. There is no other way.

"Faith is believing in God in spite of appearances."
Adrian Rogers

Day 7

Turning the Table on the Devil

You say, "I am allowed to do anything"—but not everything is good for you. And even though "I am allowed to do anything, I must not become a slave to anything."
1 Corinthians 6:12

One of Satan's most deceptive tools is the tool of distraction. If he can keep you distracted, you have little time for genuine relationships with God or others. What if you took his own strategy and strategically turned it against him? How, you ask? Consider a few life-altering decisions you could make in efforts to turn the scheme of Satan on its head:

1. What if you made a commitment that you would not allow yourself to check your email before you checked your "He-mail?" Your Bible is the message He has personally sent to you each morning. Use the urge to check your messages as a reminder to first get into the Word.

2. What if you made a commitment to pray for each person you text? Go ahead and send your text and then take the next minute to pray specifically for the person you just texted. If you know them well enough to text with them, I would think you would certainly have a calling, and maybe even an obligation, to pray for them. Many times what you are texting about are personal issues and problems. Right there is your prayer prompt! Be careful, though. While personal difficulties are a natural thing to bring up to a friend over the phone, there are times that the conversation moves into the territory of gossip. If so, just delete the text and turn your so-called information into private intercession. If you are privy to something, it is for the purpose of prayer. Oswald Chambers said, "God never gives us discernment in order that we may criticize, but that we may intercede."

3. *What if you made a commitment to spend at least as much time in front of "His face" as you spend on Facebook?* It seems that we have an insatiable desire to see what is going on with everyone but God. Henry Blackaby says the secret to finding God's will is to find out what He is doing and get in on it. Finding out what God is doing is completely different from telling God what you are doing. Bob Beaudine's book *2 Chairs: The Secret That Changes Everything* invites you to meet with God in a personal way each morning by placing an empty chair in front of you during your quiet time.[1] Visualize Him in that chair having a conversation with you. Spend time asking Him questions and listening. Do this before you start scrolling to see what everyone else is doing. Try using Satan's social media distractions as reminders to connect to God, and you will beat the devil at his own game.

> *"Good things become bad things when they keep you from the best things."*
> **Adrian Rogers**

Day 8

Into the Unknown

> *The LORD had said to Abram, "Leave your native country, your relatives, and your father's family, and go to the land that I will show you. I will make you into a great nation. I will bless you and make you famous, and you will be a blessing to others."*
> Genesis 12:1–2

The uncertainty that precedes obedience is what makes faith, faith. But the difference between blind faith and God faith is that although you are stepping into an unknown future, you are trusting a known God. You may be in the dark about your destination, but you are never in the dark regarding God's love, protection, and goodness. You are not stepping out because of a hunch; you are stepping out because you heard from Him. And when He is the One who tells you to go, even in darkness you can operate with complete certainty.

Most of the time God won't illuminate the next step until you step on the one before. Your obedience should be based on God's character and His past provision. If you knew all the turns, it wouldn't be faith. It would be a map. Don't wait for all the lights to turn green before you leave the driveway. Just know your first turn and then venture into the unknown. Charles Stanley said, "Obey God and leave all the consequences to Him."

In my experience, when I know the outcome, I find myself just going through the motions. A certain formula is completely different from radical faith. Faith doesn't have any idea where it is going to end up. Don't think of it as frightening. Think of it as thrilling. Faith is an unscripted life of unlimited prospects and potential.

If God were to say, "I'm showing up at your house tonight, and I want you to dress up," how would you feel? Would you get goose bumps if He blindfolded you and instructed you not to take it off until you arrived at the secret destination? I suspect your heart would beat out of your chest. This is who God is! He is a God of mystery, awe, and anticipation. He is full of wonders beyond anything we can imagine. What could be more fantastic than going on faith adventures with Him?

"When Abraham went out, he didn't know why, he didn't know where, he only knew whom. If your life is dull and insipid, perhaps you ought to do what Abraham did and live by faith. It will turn the monotonous to the momentous."
Adrian Rogers

Day 9

Are You Stressed over Money?

*Once I was young, and now I am old. Yet I have never seen
the godly abandoned or their children begging for bread.*
Psalm 37:25

Have you felt stressed or been guilty of acting "stressed out"? One is the result of an event. The other is just an attitude. I have experienced both. I remember a day when I was looking at my bank account, rather than my God. Instead of remaining discouraged, I stopped and made a good choice. I decided to say—out loud—all the recent things God had done to provide for me.

I recited all the gifts God had given to me through other people. It amazed me how many there were when I put them all together. I recited things I purchased, but they didn't end up costing as much as I thought they would. I recited things I was going to buy but ended up not needing. That's the same as windfall profit! I recited income that came in above what I was anticipating. I recited checks that just showed up in the mail. I recited times when I exercised willpower and changed my mind about purchasing. It seemed I had money flowing from every direction. My attitude completely changed. My stress went away. It not only went away, but it was replaced by an attitude of gratitude. Perspective!

I realized my stress was an emotion that was masking the twin sins of unbelief and ungratefulness. Has Satan duped you into thinking God has forgotten you when in reality God has been providing for you every single day? He has been providing in so many different ways. God may be allowing you to save money instead of giving you money. You may fall short of your need in your paycheck, but it may be balanced by a financial blessing in another area. When you pull back and look at things from a higher perspective, you can see the complete picture. God has indeed provided for you. God will provide for you. He is your Father, and He will always take care of His children. Sarah Ban Breathnach said, "When we choose not to focus on what is missing from our lives but are grateful for the abundance that is present . . . we experience Heaven on earth."²

> *"We trust God for spiritual things, but then we can't trust Him for material things. We can trust Him for all eternity, but we can't trust Him for tomorrow."*
> **Adrian Rogers**

Day 10

Open My Eyes, Lord

"There are more on our side than on theirs!"
2 Kings 6:16b

Have you ever felt like you were surrounded on all sides with no way to escape? Have there been days when in your wildest imagination you couldn't conjure up a possible solution for your problems? Have you felt that no matter where you turned you encountered something bigger and stronger than you? Have you felt like every single door was bolted shut? Did you know that God is the One who orchestrates it all? He does it so you have nowhere to turn but to Him. Only in giving up are you forced to look up. When you look up, He gets the glory.

The author of 2 Kings tells the story of the king of Aram. He sent a great army with many horses and chariots to surround the city to kill the prophet Elisha and his servant. Second Kings 6:15 says, "When the servant of the man of God got up early the next morning and went outside, there were horses and chariots everywhere. 'Oh, sir, what will we do now?' the young man cried to Elisha."

The story continues: "'Don't be afraid!' Elisha told him. 'For there are more on our side than on theirs!'" (2 Kings 6:16). I'm sure the servant said to Elisha, "Are you blind? Can't you see that there are warriors and horses and chariots everywhere? There are only two of us. There is no escape. This is the end." But it wasn't Elisha who was blind. It was the servant.

"Then Elisha prayed, 'O Lord, open his eyes and let him see!' The Lord opened the young man's eyes, and when he looked up, he saw that the hillside around Elisha was filled with horses and chariots of fire" (2 Kings 6:17). Chill bumps! Like Elisha's servant, may God open your eyes that you may see. The unseen world is more real than the seen world. When you feel rejection, pray that your eyes will be opened so that you can see that God has surrounded you with His love. When you feel defeat, pray that your eyes will be opened so you can see that God is protecting you with the power of the mighty hosts of heaven. When you feel despair, pray that your eyes will be opened so you will see that the victory belongs to the Lord. It is all here. Right now. May God open your eyes.

"Faith sees the invisible, believes the incredible, knows the unknowable, and receives the impossible."
Adrian Rogers

Day 11

All Relationships Are Not Created Equal

*Don't be fooled by those who say such things, for
"bad company corrupts good character."*
1 Corinthians 15:33

A deep friendship and a ministry relationship aren't the same. While some ministry relationships are two-sided, many of them tend to be one-sided, especially when you are inviting someone into your life who doesn't know the Lord or is young in their spiritual maturity and needs a great deal of your time and attention. In such relationships, it is normal for these "sprouting buds" to be needy, and possibly even toxic, people. Don't be mistaken, there are times God calls you to relate to toxic people. During those times, just give, needing nothing in return. Jesus ministered to the multitude, but Scripture says He did not "entrust himself to them" (NIV) because He "knew what was in their hearts" (John 2:24 CEV).

A genuine friendship is different. It should be reciprocal. A true friend should give back in replenishing and encouraging ways. The people you allow into your inner circle will mold your thinking. They need to be carefully selected and curated. True friendships should be two-way. If you do all the giving, it isn't a true friendship. If you receive back from a relationship, make certain that what you are receiving will make you healthier in body, soul, and spirit. Use discernment. I'm not referring to ministry opportunities with people who are hurting or poor.

Many of these people are rich in faith. There's a strong possibility they will bless you even more than you could bless them. The ones you need to beware of (when it comes to deep friendship) are toxic people. Make the distinction between toxic people and hurting people. Wear your spiritual armor around toxic people the same way you would wear a hazmat suit around a hazardous and contagious disease.

Never take spiritual counsel from a toxic person. Refuse to let a toxic person define who you are with their poisonous words. Don't allow a pessimist to discourage you. While you can certainly minister well in chaotic situations, don't shoulder all the problems created by the poor choices of others as your new problems to solve. Set boundaries. They are biblical. Yes, be a dispenser of grace. Freely give unconditional love. Speak truth into toxic people. But if it is not received, you may be "casting your pearls before swine" (see Matt. 7:6). There is always a limit because we are limited creatures. We are not God and cannot change people like He can. Many times Satan will put decoys in your path to distract and deter you from people who will be responsive. You must exercise discernment and stay tuned into the leading of the Holy Spirit. The thing you don't want to do is open yourself up to receive their toxicity back into your life. Minister to the many, but only let a few into your inner circle. A good rule is to give love *and* guard your heart. Make certain that hurting people see Jesus as their Savior, not you.

> *"One of the measurements as to whether or not that person is a real friend is this, 'Am I a better person when I am in his presence?'"*
> **Adrian Rogers**

Day 12

Other People's Needs

*What good is it, dear brothers and sisters, if you say you
have faith but don't show it by your actions.*
James 2:14

Is your attention drawn to a problem? Is there a person your heart hurts for when you hear of their financial need? In John Stick's book *Follow the Cloud*, he says that whenever someone comes to him and says, "Somebody should really do something about that," his response is always the same: "You're right; you should!"[3]

Listen to me. Whatever problem you are noticing right now in someone's life, God put it on *your* heart. Many times God answers the prayers of those who hurt by placing their burdens in the hearts of the people He intends to use to answer those prayers. If you can feel their pain, oftentimes there is something you need to personally do. But before you jump out there, I feel the need to walk you through some basic principles.

1. Though you may be called to be a helper, you are not the Savior. Point people to Jesus. But when you do, don't forget that most of the time when Jesus works, He works through people. He will give you the resources to help and the desire to do it. It will come *through* you, but it will be *all* Him. The glory will go to Him. You will remain in the background.

2. If God has prompted you to act, remember that timing is important. God spends a lot of time preparing a needy person's heart to receive a miracle. The ground must be tilled before the seeds are planted. Gifts given too soon can enable the behavior that may have created the problem. God intends for the person with the need to come to a place of brokenness. If you rescue them too quickly, you may circumvent what God needs to do first.
3. If you are the one who receives the burden, in most cases it is for you to act personally, not for you to delegate. Don't take up an offering when God intends for you to be the one to write the check. He may want others to be involved, but don't neglect your part of the equation. God doesn't burden you so that you can ease your conscience by recruiting others to do the lion's share of the work.
4. Prayer is the starting point, not always the ending point. Sometimes God says, "Watch what I will do." Other times He says, "Watch what I will do through you." Burden-bearing is not a spectator sport. Intercession is volunteering, if needed, to partner with God to be the answer to someone's prayer. If that doesn't give your life meaning, I don't know what would.

"Don't give until it hurts; give until it feels good."
Adrian Rogers

Day 13

What Has God Already Told You to Do?

"So why do you keep calling me 'Lord, Lord!' when you don't do what I say?"
Luke 6:46

I can tell you how to live a simple life. Don't worry about final destinations and just focus on the next step. Just take the next step! However tiny that step may be, just do the next thing God has prompted your heart to do. If you are taking a trip, the first thing you need to do is simple. Just pull out of the driveway. If you wait on all the lights to turn green before you begin, you never will. God speaks in much the same way as a GPS. You have to be moving to get turn-by-turn directions.

I'm going to ask you an easy but painful question: Has God told you to do anything you haven't yet done? You may not receive the next instructions until you have completed the first instructions. Think about it. Why would God bother to show you something else when you haven't even done what He has already shown you?

I'll go ahead and confess. God has been telling me to write this devotional book for years. I've ignored it. I've procrastinated. Then I came to a place in my journey where I felt stuck. I didn't have a clue what God wanted me to do. I remembered that God had told me to write this book. I had no idea how I would ever complete it. To write this many different devotional thoughts, all based on scriptural truth, is overwhelming. But I finally obeyed God and pulled out of the driveway.

When I began to write the first one, it was like the directions for all the other areas in my life just started to flow. That one act of disobedience, that I conveniently called procrastination, was clogging up everything. I realized that the silence in my spirit wasn't because God wasn't speaking. It was because God had already spoken, and He was waiting on my reply.

What has God already told you to do? Sin isn't just doing what you shouldn't do. Sin is also not doing what you should do. One is a sin of commission. The other is a sin of omission. They are both sins. You complete the tasks God is calling you to by taking one simple, small step after another. "Even the snails eventually reached the ark!" I couldn't see how I was ever going to finish all the devotions in this book. I did it by just focusing on the next one.

"You can't steer a ship that isn't moving."
Adrian Rogers

Day 14

It's All in How You Say It

He will not fight or shout or raise His voice in public. He will not crush the weakest reed or put out a flickering candle.
Matthew 12:19–20

Do you seem to offend someone every time you open your mouth? If so, you may want to consider the possibility that the problem may not be the other person's easily offended nature. The problem may be you. I heard Pastor Kenny Grant say, "If everywhere you go, there are issues, is you!" You would have to hear the adorable way he says it to really get it. But there is a strong possibility that you are the problem. Do you feel that you are called to be a "culture warrior" in a deceived world who needs to drop "truth bombs" everywhere, especially on social media? Let me ask: Is your goal to expose wrong or to win people to Christ? Bashing people with biblical truth won't soften hearts; it will only alienate them.

To speak truth into a godless world, people have a better chance of receiving what you have to say if you say it in a way that they can understand and grapple with. Here's a wonderful checklist I found that can equip you to share in a way that opens hearts: tone, tact, and timing.

Tone. Most of the time, it is more about how you say something than what you actually say. It is amazing what you *are* able to say if you say it in a gentle way with a soft voice and a smile on your face. If you can physically touch the person, that can help too.

Tact. Trust me. You can always say the same thing in much more palatable terms. If you know something is going to be difficult, then write it out, pray it through, edit it, run it past someone you trust, and then edit it again. There is always a better way to say the same thing. If have a weaponized tongue like me, it may take three or four edits.

Timing. If you don't get this right, then what you say will not be received, even if it is gentle and thoroughly edited. Don't say something hard to hear in the midst of stress. It will never be received well. "Like apples of gold in settings of silver, is a word spoken at the proper time" (Prov. 25:11 NASB).

"Sometimes people irritate me, and the old Adrian in me has a tendency just to tell them where to get off. But I can't do that. That's somebody for whom Jesus died, and I don't want to say anything or be anything or do anything that could keep me from sharing the love of God with that person."
Adrian Rogers

Day 15

God's Gift Closet

How great is the goodness You have stored up for those who fear You. You lavish it on those who come to You for protection, blessing them before the watching world.
Psalm 31:19

Is there anyone who doesn't love to spoil their grandchildren? The joy of my life is to have a special surprise for mine every time they visit. And the more excited they are to come, the more excited I am to give them something they will love. I know some grandparents who make a run through the toy section even when they go to the grocery store! If those little ones are causing a strain on your budget, I can give you a hint. My grandson is just as happy when I find a rock for him in the yard. He's still young. I'm sure he will catch on soon, and I'll be financially ruined!

He really loves cars. He doesn't know it, but I have an entire bucket of cars in my closet. If his parents didn't stop me, I would give him a new Matchbox car for every day of the year. They are stored and waiting. You are like that, too. When you see things your precious grandchildren will love, I know you buy them and put them in your closet. My closet contains planes and rockets, cars and trucks. There are stuffed animals, plastic animals, and even mechanical animals. I'm beginning to sound like Bubba Gump listing ways to cook shrimp! Inside my closet there are dolls and dresses and cowboys and costumes.

Use your imagination to think of the content of God's gift closet and the things He has put back for you when you come to visit. Matthew 7:11 says, "So if you sinful people know how to give good gifts to your children, how much more will your heavenly Father give good gifts to those who ask Him." God can't wait to lavish you with the good gifts He has carefully selected with your desires in mind. He isn't waiting on Christmas or your birthday. This is a daily thing. All He is waiting on is for you to expectantly come into His presence. When you don't come, you don't receive. It's that simple. You also don't receive when you come with a self-centered wish list. When you do that, your wise Father knows that what you need most is some work on your character. But when you come because you love to be with Him, you'll never be disappointed by the gift in His hand.

"God is waiting for me to wait for Him."
Adrian Rogers

Day 16

Run for Your Life

*"Find Jehu son of Jehoshaphat, son of Nimshi. Call him into a private room away from his friends, and pour the oil over his head. Say to him, 'This is what the L*ORD* says: I anoint you to be the king over Israel.' Then open the door and run for your life!"*
2 Kings 9:2–3

Your assignment might be to do exactly what God tells you to do and then "run for your life!" Few people will love you for telling them the truth. The apostle Paul said in Galatians 4:16, "Have I now become your enemy because I am telling you the truth?" Many times you are going to have to run for your life for delivering the exact message God told you to deliver.

We've all heard that "He who would have friends must show himself friendly" (Prov. 18:24). But it is also true that "he who would have enemies speaks the truth." A godly man is known for both the people who love him and the people who hate him. When you die, you don't want the minister to say, "She was loved by everyone." Paul said in 2 Timothy 4:3–5,

> For a time is coming when people will no longer listen to sound and wholesome teaching. They will follow their own desires and will look for teachers who will tell them whatever their itching ears want to hear. They will reject the truth and chase after myths. But you should keep a clear mind in every situation. Don't

be afraid of suffering for the Lord. Work at telling others the Good News, and fully carry out the ministry God has given you.

I am here to tell you that the time is no longer coming. The time is here right now!

People today cower in fear of the retribution they will receive for speaking up. Paul said, "Don't be afraid of suffering!" If you don't have enemies, you aren't delivering the message. Second Timothy 3:12 says, "Yes, and everyone who wants to live a godly life in Christ Jesus will suffer persecution." Sometimes you just need to say what God has told you to say and run for your life.

Where do you run? Run to the Rock! Psalm 18:2–3 tells us, "The LORD is My rock, in whom I find protection. He is my shield, the power that saves me, and my place of safety. I called on the LORD, who is worthy of praise, and He saved me from my enemies."

"When people meet me, I need to duck or pucker because I know they are either going to take a swing at me or kiss me."
Adrian Rogers

Day 17

A Grace Vending Machine

*If indeed you have heard of the stewardship of God's
grace which was given to me for you.*
Ephesians 3:2 (NASB)

When you think about stewardship, most of you think about money. And no doubt you are to be faithful with God's money. But Ephesians 3 tells us that there is an additional kind of stewardship. It is "the stewardship of God's grace."

Paul was made a "steward of God's grace" so that he might be the dispenser of it on behalf of God to others. And, as a steward of God's grace, Paul goes on to say what he prays for them:

> I pray that from His glorious, unlimited resources He will empower you with inner strength through His Spirit. Then Christ will make His home in your hearts as you trust in Him. Your roots will grow down into God's love and keep you strong. And may you have the power to understand, as all God's people should, how wide, how long, how high, and how deep His love is. May you experience the love of Christ, though it is too great to understand fully. Then you will be made complete with all the fullness of life and power that comes from God. (Eph. 3:16–19)

Wow! As a "steward of God's grace," you have the incredible privilege of dispensing that grace to others. You get to speak truth into their life. You get to be His hands and feet. You can choose to be a "grace vending machine" who provides refreshment to the souls of others God has entrusted to your care. You can pray for your loved ones. Insert their name into this prayer in Ephesians 3. There is nothing more powerful than praying Scripture. If you pray Scripture, you can be positive you are praying the will of God!

Because you are a steward, you don't own this grace. You don't have to manufacture it. God provides it. You just manage and dispense it on His behalf. Whom can you think of that needs God's grace today? You have been entrusted with His grace to give! As a matter of fact, if you don't give it away, He won't give you more to dispense. That is the essence of stewardship.

> *"The greatest greatness is not to be great but to make others great."*
> **Adrian Rogers**

Day 18

Are You Qualified?

It is not that we think we are qualified to do anything on our own. Our qualification comes from God.
2 Corinthians 3:5

Have you ever applied for a job and been told you weren't qualified? Right now, I am writing the devotional book you are reading. Yet I don't think I'm qualified to write it. Actually, I'm not only not qualified; I'm terrified. It would be easy for me to write a book about reasons I shouldn't write a book. That book would flow out of me.

So, why haven't I written this until now? It's simple. I have been afraid. When I pick up other devotional books, I always come to the same conclusion: "Gayle, you aren't good enough." "It has already been written by someone who says it far better than you." "Why embarrass yourself?" "You aren't Oswald Chambers. You know Adrian Rogers and you certainly aren't him!" There's an additional aspect to, "I'm not good enough." It's that I am afraid I'm not good enough as a person. I have repeated failures. In many ways I feel like a hypocrite. I struggle. All I do is write about those struggles.

Here is the big question: Has God told you to do something? I'm telling you (and I am telling me) with 100-percent certainty that *if God* has indeed told you to do it, you most certainly *can* do it. You can do it *if* you let Christ do it through you. You see, when that happens, it is not you who is doing it. It is Christ doing it through you. Philippians 4:13

says, "For I can do everything through Christ, who gives me strength." So remember, *you* really can't. But *He* can.

There are only two parameters to being able to do anything. They are: Did God, indeed, tell you to do it? And are you allowing God to do it through you? You are the glove. He is the hand. Without the hand, the glove is powerless. But with the hand inside, the glove can do anything the hand can do. God will never tell you to do anything He will not empower you to do. Don't trust yourself to be able. Trust Him. You aren't qualified by your own credentials. You are using His credentials. Just do it!

In my case, I have an escape. Just in case I'm not any good, I'm putting a quote from my dad at the end of each page. I know that what he says will be!

"There are plenty of people who can preach the gospel better than me, but there is no one who can preach a better gospel than me."
Adrian Rogers

Day 19

Vive la Différence

"But 'God made them male and female'
from the beginning of creation."
Mark 10:6

It has always been true, and it will always be true. Men and women are different. The difference between men and women helps the world see many things about God in a broad sense, but when we narrow in on marriage specifically, we see that the relationship between husband and wife is intended to be a picture to the lost world of Jesus Christ and His relationship with His bride, the church. Husbands and wives are different because we have the high privilege of acting out God's heavenly drama on the stage of our homes.

These roles in marriage may never be reversed. The husband is always the one who plays the role of Christ, bearing the responsibilities of being an authority, nurturer, cherisher, self-sacrifcer, and lover over the wife (Eph. 5:25–30). How does he picture this daily? By laying down his life for her every chance he gets. Why? Because he is a picture and type of Christ, who is the church's nurturer, cherisher, lover, and authority! He's the one who laid down His life for us. Husbands follow His lead. The wife is always in subjection to the husband because she is a picture and type of the church, who submits to Christ. How does she picture this daily? By respecting her husband every chance she gets (Eph. 5:33). These roles have nothing to do with one spouse having more ability, intelligence, or spirituality compared to the other. It has everything to do with the greater story God is telling through marriage—the story of His Son and His people (see Eph. 5:22–33).

Let me assure you that if you are a female and married, your role as a wife is far from degrading. Playing this role is fulfilling God's calling for you. Your greatest fulfillment should be when you can say, "I press toward the mark for . . . the high calling of God in Christ Jesus" (Phil. 3:14 KJV). Acting out a role God has not assigned to you is when you lose your identity. How backward today's thinking has become. Satan is behind it all. Why? Because he hates the relationship ordinary marriages point to—the love relationship between Christ and the church. He is the one who wants wives to act like husbands and husbands to act like wives. I can't blame the lost world for being confused. They have no understanding of the picture they are portraying.

The traditional concepts of marriage (and some could say, gender) are being carefully and deliberately dismantled because degrading marriage destroys the picture of Christ as our head, our lover and nurturer, and Lord, and the church who joyfully submits to His lordship. You and I can't change God's plan. It is a good plan. Genesis 1:27–28a, 31 says, "So God created human beings in His image. In the image of God He created them; male and female He created them. Then God blessed them and said, 'Be fruitful and multiply.' . . . Then God looked over all He had made, and He saw that it was very good!"

> *"A woman is infinitely superior to a man . . . at being a woman. And a man is infinitely superior to a woman . . . at being a man."*
> **Adrian Rogers**

Day 20

The Right Goal

For everything comes from Him and exists by His power and is intended for His glory. All glory to Him forever! Amen.
Romans 11:36

Is your heart full of restlessness? You know that Jesus said, "I am come that they might have life, and that they may have it more abundantly" (John 10:10 NKJV). But you still feel empty. On top of that, you feel guilty about feeling empty. Instead of being "filled with the Spirit," you are not filled with anything but soul hunger.

Obviously, you want what Jesus has to offer. But wanting it doesn't always translate into a life of abundance. The problem lies in the fact that you have a firmly rooted false belief about what will fill those empty places in your heart. So you numb yourself with constant activity and overachievement. Yet no matter how you excel on the outside, there is always a deep longing on the inside. This isn't going to change if your reason for living is wrong. No matter how good it may seem, you can't satisfy your emptiness with anything in this world. The only thing God unequivocally promises from this world is that "in this world you will have trouble" (John 16:33b NIV).

If your goal is to bring glory to Jesus, there is always hope. You may experience a wonderful marriage, godly children, financial freedom, robust health, and total happiness. God longs to bless you with these things. But He can't promise them to you on this earth because we live in a fallen, sinful world, and He refuses to violate the free will of the people with whom you live. Your "confident hope" comes from "what God has reserved for you in heaven" (Col. 1:5). Heaven is the only place where there are no tears or sorrow. The beautiful thing is that the blackest of your life circumstances always give you the best background to display the grace of God. And God's grace and God's glory are what it's all about. God is not nearly as interested in changing your circumstances as He is in using your circumstances to change you. That is what will bring Him glory.

> *"Your heart should not be consumed with the gifts of God but with the glory of God."*
> **Adrian Rogers**

Day 21

Even Though

Even though the fig trees have no blossoms, and there are no grapes on the vines . . . yet I will rejoice in the LORD! I will be joyful in the God of my salvation!
Habakkuk 3:17a–18

Oh, if we could have an "even though" faith. Actually, that is exactly what faith is. Faith is believing something we cannot see. It is even beyond that. It is believing things that are contrary to what we see. Hebrews 11:1 says, "Faith is the confidence that what we hope for will actually happen; it gives us assurance about things we cannot see." If you could see it, it wouldn't be faith. Faith requires the unknown and the unseen. Faith honors God because it involves trust in who He is.

Your joy does not come as a result of earthly fortune or prosperity. Habakkuk said that joy is in God, not in gifts. This passage is one for you to memorize. You have to carry these verses inside of you!

> Even though the fig trees have no blossoms, and there are no grapes on the vines; even though the olive crop fails, and the fields lie empty and barren; even though the flocks die in the fields, and the cattle barns are empty, yet I will rejoice in the LORD! I will be joyful in the God of my salvation! The Sovereign LORD is my strength! He makes me as surefooted as a deer, able to tread upon the heights. (Hab. 3:17–19)

It reminds me of what Job said after God gave Satan permission to take away everything he held dear. He still proclaimed: "Though He slay me, yet will I trust Him" (Job 13:15a NKJV).

It reminds me of what the three Hebrew boys, Shadrach, Meshach, and Abednego, said to Nebuchadnezzar when they were told to bow down to him or be thrown into the fiery furnace. They said, "If we are thrown into the blazing furnace, the God whom we serve is able to save us. He will rescue us from your power, Your Majesty. But even if He doesn't, we want to make it clear to you, Your Majesty, that we will never serve your gods or worship the gold statue you have set up" (Dan. 3:17–18).

Do you have an "even though" faith? If your treasure is in the things of this world, you won't have this kind of faith. Matthew 6:20–21 says, "Store your treasures in heaven, where moths and rust cannot destroy, and thieves do not break in and steal. Wherever your treasure is, there the desires of your heart will also be." Ephesians 1:3 says, "All praise to God, the Father of our Lord Jesus Christ, who has blessed us with every spiritual blessing in the heavenly realms because we are united with Christ."

"True riches are in the realm of the spiritual—they must be because the spiritual is the only thing that's going to last."
Adrian Rogers

Day 22

The Whole Truth and Nothing but the Truth

Some of you were once like that. But you were cleansed; you were made holy; you were made right with God.
1 Corinthians 6:11

Many times self-righteous people quote portions of Scripture without giving the whole picture of redemption that the entirety of Scripture presents. To share the condemnation for certain types of sins without sharing God's accompanying grace and provision for that sin is not a complete truth. Many things are accepted and celebrated in today's culture that are abhorrent to the Holy God of the Bible. Sin is graphically exposed in the Bible in order to show our desperate need for a Savior. The truth that certain things are sin is still truth. God never tiptoes around that. But He also never fails to offer hope and grace to the sinners.

I love that 1 Corinthians 6:9–11 says:

> Don't you realize that those who do wrong will not inherit the Kingdom of God? Don't fool yourselves. Those who indulge in sexual sin, or who worship idols, or commit adultery, or are male prostitutes, or practice homosexuality, or are thieves or greedy people, or drunkards, or are abusive, or cheat people—none of these will inherit the Kingdom of God. Some of you

were once like that. But you were cleansed; you were made holy; you were made right with God by calling on the name of the Lord Jesus Christ and by the Spirit of our God.

God would never call something a sin and then create some people in sinful ways that they could not change. Sin is clearly stated. But don't miss this. Then it says: "Some of you were once like that." *Were*, as in, past tense. In every category Paul lists, there are saints who were "once like that." Don't let anyone tell you there is anything you can't change. They are now cleansed, made holy, and made right with God. Hallelujah!

Never condemn the sin without pointing to the Savior. The entire Bible is a story of man's falling short of God's perfection and the redemption He provides in Jesus that completely covers those sins as if they never happened.

Do you still feel guilty and unworthy, when God has cleansed you and made you holy? That guilt isn't from God. Satan is the only source of condemnation for something that has been forgiven and forsaken.

"If you take part of the truth, and try to make that part of the truth, all of the truth, then that part of the truth becomes an untruth."
Adrian Rogers

Day 23

You Can Learn to Speak a New Language

Kind words are like honey—sweet to the soul and healthy for the body.
Proverbs 16:24

How much would the atmosphere of your home change if a guard could be placed over your mouth that made it impossible for an impatient or unkind word to pass through? That would be a greater invention than the doggie gate! It might turn your home into a palace.

Is it possible for you to say the same thing in a softer, gentler way? As I write this devotional, I am constantly thinking about how I can phrase something in a better way. What if *you* became your own editor? Proverbs 15:28 says, "The heart of the godly thinks carefully before speaking." What could you say that would be encouraging or uplifting? How could you make the person you are talking to feel better about who they are and what they are going through? It requires intentionality.

Never forget that when someone is rude, it is simply an indication that they have an empty emotional tank. Instead of responding *in kind*, what would happen if you responded by *being kind*? Make it your life goal to pour kindness into empty tanks. Respond instead of react. This one change will be transformative. People will notice. They will be drawn to you like a magnet. As a by-product, when you fill their previously love-starved emotional tank, hopefully, they will begin to reciprocate some of that patience and kindness back your way. You may not be a great theologian or a brilliant scholar, but you can understand these five simple words: "Love is patient and kind" (1 Cor. 13:4). You can begin to live them. It starts by comparing every word that comes out of your mouth by that standard.

"There are a lot of folk who are religious but not necessarily kind. That's the reason a little girl prayed, 'Lord, make all the bad people good and all the good people nice.'"
Adrian Rogers

Day 24

Because You Are United in Christ

*God has united you with Christ Jesus. For our benefit God
made Him to be wisdom itself. Christ made us right with God;
He made us pure and holy, and He freed us from sin.*
1 Corinthians 1:30

You are blessed with every spiritual blessing in the heavenlies because you are united with Christ. There is nothing you need that you don't already possess! "All praise to God, the Father of our Lord Jesus Christ, who has blessed us with every spiritual blessing in the heavenly realms because we are united with Christ" (Eph. 1:3).

You have received an inheritance from God because you are united with Christ. You are literally co-inheritors with the Son of God. Unfathomable! "Furthermore, because we are united with Christ, we have received an inheritance from God, for He chose us in advance, and He makes everything work out according to His plan" (Eph. 1:11).

You are raised from the dead and seated in the heavenlies because you are united with Christ. Because you entered into His death, you also received the same power that raised Him from the dead: "For he raised us from the dead along with Christ and seated us with Him in the heavenly realms because we are united with Christ Jesus" (Eph. 2:6).

You receive the same love and affection He gives to His Son because you are united with Christ. God loves you the same way He loves Jesus: "So God can point to us in all future ages as examples of the incredible wealth of His grace and kindness toward us, as shown in all He has done for us who are united with Christ Jesus" (Eph. 2:7).

You have been reconciled to God and have a sure and certain hope because you are united with Christ: "You lived in this world without God and without hope. But now you have been united with Christ Jesus. Once you were far away from God, but now you have been brought near to him through the blood of Christ." (Eph. 2:12b–13).

You are so completely bound to Him that nothing can separate you. You are in Him and He is in you. What is true of Him is true of you. You share in all that He is. The same power that lives in Him lives in you. Everything that is His is yours. This mystery is divine truth. Through Christ, you are adopted into God's family with all its rights and privileges!

"Jesus became forever like me that I might become forever like Him."
Adrian Rogers

Day 25

The Lion King

Stay alert! Watch out for your great enemy, the devil. He prowls around like a roaring lion, looking for someone to devour.
1 Peter 5:8

He was born to be a king, the rightful heir to the throne, but he believes the lies of his Uncle Scar, who orders him to run away in disgrace and shame. He flees from his calling and kingdom to live a life of insignificance, eating bugs with a silly meerkat and a stinking warthog. Simba, who was called to be a king, piddles away his time singing "Hakuna Matata."

I find it significant that his uncle was named Scar. There is another Scar, another lion who roams about: "Stay alert! Watch out for your great enemy, the devil. He prowls around like a roaring lion, looking for someone to devour" (1 Pet. 5:8). Like young Simba, don't let the "scars" in your life define you. Don't let your scars rob you of your birthright. Don't allow your scars to keep you from your calling. Don't let them destroy the impact on the kingdom God has created you to make.

For most of my life, I have felt like my Enemy, the devil, aka Scar, has duped me into believing that I am not good enough, I am not worthy, and I can't be used. Through his lies, he has banished me to a wilderness existence of eating bugs and singing "Hakuna Matata." Has the same thing happened to you? Have you forgotten who you are? Are you following meerkats and warthogs, making you believe this is the life for which you were destined when your Father is the King of kings?

At one point the monkey, Rafiki, hits Simba in the head with a stick. Simba asks him: "Why did you do that?" Rafiki replies: "It doesn't matter. It's in the past." Like Rafiki, I'm here to hit you in the head and tell you that whatever you have done, whatever scars you carry, it is in the past. It's time to move forward. It's time to reclaim your birthright. You are a child of God and coheir with Jesus. Satan has made you feel like you are nothing for long enough. It is a lie. He lies because he knows that if you ever remember who you are and embrace what God has called you to do, his unlawful reign will come to an untimely end.

"When we bring our wounds to Jesus and let Him heal them, our scars may become our greatest ministry."
Adrian Rogers

Day 26

But It's So Hard!

I have worked hard and long, enduring many sleepless nights. I have been hungry and thirsty and have often gone without food. I have shivered in the cold, without enough clothing to keep me warm.
2 Corinthians 11:27

Most people think life is only good when times are easy. They associate God's blessings with Him clearing out resistance and unlocking doors. Unfortunately, little growth takes place when life is easy. Muscle growth only comes from resistance. If God gives us good times and smooth pathways, it is probably because He knows we will need the rest for the tedious journey and hard-earned progress that lies ahead.

Where do you find yourself? Do you feel that God has forsaken you because your cushy life has taken a hard left turn? Do you assume that the difficulties of your situation are God's redirections? Years ago I took a trip with a friend. I asked her to do something, and she replied in a whiney tone, "But it's so hard." There was just something about the way she said it that makes me repeat it in the same tone whenever there is something I don't want to do. I laugh about the memory every time it comes out of my mouth. But some times are really hard. Soldier up!

Quit questioning whether God wants you to do what He has clearly told you to do. Difficulty doesn't change the assignment. It may make it more challenging. But the more challenging the task, the more fulfilling the result. Many things you are called to do are true labors of love.

Since life can be hard, aren't you glad you aren't in this life alone? First of all, Jesus knows your load is heavy. He tells you to give it to Him and let Him carry it. "Give your burdens to the LORD, and he will take care of you" (Ps. 55:22a). Second, He made you for companionship. You have friends who will look out for you: "Share each other's burdens, and in this way obey the law of Christ" (Gal. 6:2). When you are tired, I will take your burden. When I get tired, you take mine. It's hard, but you can do it. You have Jesus and we have each other.

"Peace is not the subtraction of problems; it is the addition of power to meet those problems."
Adrian Rogers

Day 27

You Might Be the Cause of Your Own Problems

Do all that you can to live in peace with everyone.
Romans 12:18

When someone is critical of you, always consider these three possibilities:

First, ask yourself, *Is there any truth to what this person has said about me?* If so, confess it to God, and confess it to the person you have offended. Then change. No one cares about your confession if there is no change in your behavior. And you not only need to change, but you may need to make restitution. For instance, if someone steals something, they need to confess it and not steal again. They also need to return what they stole.

Second, ask yourself, *Do I have a blind spot?* If it is truly a blind spot, you won't be aware of it. Thus, it is called a blind spot! You certainly won't realize it's a big deal. In that case, humbly ask the opinion of someone you admire if there could be any truth in this accusation. If you can't see it, but your trusted friend concurs, then confess it, change, and if needed, make restitution.

Third, if the first two questions are a no, then you need to ask, *Does the criticizer have a need?* If you sincerely went through the first two questions with no guilt on your part, then you need to let their criticism roll off you like water off a duck's back. Proverbs 26:2 says, "Like a fluttering sparrow or a darting swallow, an undeserved curse will not land on its intended victim." You may not have a problem, but the person making the accusation has a need. They have responded out of emptiness or bitterness. An empty person needs to be filled with unconditional love. A bitter person needs to be sweetened with grace.

My prayer is that these simple questions will help you sort out and deal with your potential relational issues. You won't be able to fix all of them, but you will be able to fix most of them. Romans 12:18 says, "Do all that you can to live in peace with everyone." Most translations say, "If it be possible." You have to do what you can do. But you don't have to do more than you can do. From there, it is between them and God.

"What some people call 'burying the hatchet' is just digging up more dirt."
Adrian Rogers

Day 28

Ministry or Manipulation?

*People may be pure in their own eyes,
but the LORD examines their motives.*
Proverbs 16:2

It's time to check your motives! Did you know it is possible to fool yourself into thinking that you are ministering to someone when all you are doing is trying to manipulate them to do something for you? You are trying to subtly obligate them. They may not discern your motives immediately, but they will eventually. You can't make a lasting impact if people don't think you genuinely care about them. It has been said that people do not care how much you know until they know how much you care. That can be adapted to say that people do not care how much you do for them if they don't think you really care.

Manipulation says, "You exist to do something for me, and I'm going to do whatever it takes to get you to do it. If I have to be kind to get you to do it, I will be kind. But my ultimate goal is not to encourage you; my ultimate goal is to get you to do what I want you to do." I wrote a great poem, (feel free to submit it for me if you know of any poetry contests, ha!): "You might bake a cake, but you're a fake. A good deed does not a minister make." It's all in your motive!

On the other hand, genuine ministry is when you stop trying to get something from someone and start trying to give something to someone. Ministry is when you do the things that will make them a better person, things that will enrich their life. Don't ask, "What do you have that I can get?" but, "What do you need that I can give?" Manipulation subtracts. Ministry adds. Manipulation uses. Ministry gives. Here's the trick. Many times it is the same action. It's the motive that makes the difference. The person you are doing something for will eventually be able to discern that motive.

When someone is convinced you genuinely love them and have their welfare before your own, they will do more to reciprocate on their own than you ever could have manipulated them into reciprocating. Unconditional love is a motivating force. For me personally, I will move mountains for someone who loves me that way.

*"We are to love people and use things,
not love things and use people."*
Adrian Rogers

Day 29

Check-Ins for Schedule Review

We must quickly carry out the tasks assigned us by the One who sent us. The night is coming, and then no one can work.
John 9:4

Martin Luther famously said, "I have so much to do that I shall spend the first three hours in prayer."⁴ Time waiting on God is never lost. And time is never gained by diving in immediately.

My father frequently said, "There is enough time in every day to do *gracefully* everything God intends for you to do." There is a lot in that statement. There definitely isn't enough time to do everything everyone but God expects you to do each day. The problem is that you do not check in with Him for schedule review in the morning. Then you frantically go through your day with a wide-open calendar letting anyone who wants to write anything on it they desire.

God must be the one to set your agenda. If He doesn't, someone else will. Or, worse yet, you will have no agenda at all, and you will be an easy target for all the delegators and dumpers of the world. Do you realize that most people you come into contact with during the day have their own agenda? And they would love to use you to help them accomplish that agenda for them. If you aren't careful, you will spend your entire day responding to the urgent agenda of everyone but God. People are looking for someone without any sense of Divine direction. They love folks who are incapable of saying no because they find their self-worth in the opinions of others. It is good to remember the well-worn quote, "The need is not the call." Many things need to be done but not necessarily by you. Words cloaked in spiritual lingo do not assure that the speaker is God.

God does have specific desires for you each day. But you won't hear what they are if you don't seek His face and tune into His voice. He should be the One to pass out your assignments. Only when you plan your life with God's direction will you be free to say no to the distractions that are carefully planted by Satan to keep you from your true calling. If you don't, you will end up like a stadium beach ball that changes direction with every person who touches it.

"There is enough time in every day to do gracefully everything God intends for you to do."
Adrian Rogers

Day 30

Are Successful People Successful?

*"So those who are last now will be first then,
and those who are first will be last."*
Matthew 20:16

The answer to that question is: "It depends." Some are, some aren't. There are certain professions where it can be difficult to be at the very top without violating other priorities to get there. If you are judging success in relation to other people, there are too many people you are judging yourself against who may be willing to do anything to be at the top. You may have to outperform people who do not care about serving, relationships, or worship. You may have to outperform people who neglect their families. You may have to outperform people who compromise their health. You may have to outperform people who are willing to step on and over anyone or anything that gets in their way. The things I have listed are the profiles of some people who are number one in their profession. This profile is the type of person you may have to beat out for that top position, and worse still, that is the person you could become in the process of doing so.

Furthermore, if this is the person you become in the process, then your life is not a success. It is a colossal failure. Proverbs 14:12 warns: "There is a path before each person that seems right, but it ends in death." James 3:16 says, "For wherever there is jealousy and selfish ambition, there you will find disorder and evil of every kind." This verse tells me that if you arrive at your desired destination in the wrong way, your relationships and your life could end up in a complete and total mess.

Praise God, there is another way. Just as Scripture says the first will be last, it also says the last will be first. The way up is down. The way up is through humility, service, and putting the needs of others before your own. When you take care of God's business, He will take care of yours. Matthew 6:33 promises: "Seek the Kingdom of God above all else, and live righteously, and He will give you everything you need." First Chronicles 29:12 says, "Wealth and honor come from You alone, for You rule over everything. Power and might are in Your hand, and at Your discretion people are made great and given strength."

True success is found in your character, not in your position. Keep in mind that if God can trust you to use it for His glory, He may give you a position of great influence. If God can trust you as a steward, He may give you enough riches to generously share. But those things will come as a by-product of seeking Him, not from what the Bible calls selfish ambition. When you do your work for God's glory, you will find that your success will be the by-product of doing it God's way.

"Is what I'm living for worth Christ dying for?"
Adrian Rogers

Day 31

Building on the Right Foundation

"Anyone who listens to My teaching and follows it is wise, like a person who builds a house on solid rock. Though the rain comes in torrents and the floodwaters rise and the winds beat against that house, it won't collapse because it is built on bedrock. But anyone who hears My teaching and doesn't obey it is foolish, like a person who builds a house on sand. When the rains and floods come and the winds beat against that house, it will collapse with a mighty crash."
Matthew 7:24–27

People believe the lies of a godless world and the brainwashing of godless institutions because their roots aren't deep and their foundation isn't solid. They are gullible targets for any perversion of truth. They are susceptible to any storm. Being a Christian does not keep you from poison-tipped darts in the form of doubt and deception from Satan. Rather, it makes you the target of them. Being a Christian does not keep you from storms in the way of trials and sorrows. They come to everyone. But it does give you a foundation that will be able to experience the onslaughts of hell and still stand firm.

We are living in a post-Christian society which has less and less tolerance for the public proclamation of biblical truth. I implore you to saturate your entire mind, soul, and spirit with the teaching of God's Word from bold proclaimers of truth while there is opportunity. If you are listening to valueless pop music or mindless chatter on your radio as you commute to work, you are missing a major window of opportunity that God has provided. I beg you to memorize large portions of Scripture. Do not take being able to legally own a Bible in the future for granted. You must prepare. You must make it a priority.

David Allan Coe said, "The success of high-rise buildings across the world is because of their strong foundations. The deeper and stronger the foundations, the easier it will be for a building to survive the test of nature. Without the right foundations, your house or building will not last very long. It is not the beauty of a building you should look at; it's the construction of the foundation that will stand the test of time."[5]

"The only sin today is to call sin, sin."
Adrian Rogers

Day 32

How Do You Choose?

I press on to reach the end of the race and receive the heavenly prize for which God, through Christ Jesus, is calling us.
Philippians 3:14

Choosing between good and evil isn't hard. What is hard is choosing between good and best. Sometimes it is choosing between what is profitable and what isn't. Binge-watching a television series might not be forbidden in Scripture, but if you are using the only time you have to read the Scripture or spend quality time with your family, it could become sinful. Where there are two conflicting desires, the wise person chooses the desire with the most value. One of them has to go.

Maturity in Christ boils down to consistently choosing to do the most important thing. The reason we rarely choose the most important thing is because activities that have value tend to be harder to do. They require effort. Muscle isn't built without resistance. Value isn't achieved without sacrifice. Growth doesn't happen inside your comfort zone. If you want something more than you already have, you are going to have to develop some disciplines. You are going to have to make better choices. Success in life is never achieved in neutral.

Don't make it your goal to complete everything on your to-do list. A to-do list that isn't prioritized has little value. You can waste a lot of time doing things that don't even need to be done if you just do whatever the next thing might be. Marking some tasks off your list without doing them is even better than taking the time to do them. If you aren't certain about an activity, I recommend that you intentionally procrastinate it. Many times it will become apparent that it wasn't even necessary. The best use of your time might be to find a five-hundred-page novel and not read it.

Choose activities that will make you holier, healthier, and happier. Choose service over slothfulness. Choose real relationships over reality TV. Choose rising early over sleeping in. You will find the time to do the things you ought to do if you stop doing the things you shouldn't. Start now by consciously choosing the best thing. You cannot change your future without changing your today.

> *"On our list of activities in life: There are some things we need to eliminate, some things we need to delegate, and the rest we need to dedicate."*
> **Adrian Rogers**

Day 33

Pain Precedes New Birth

Weeping may last through the night, but joy comes with the morning.
Psalm 30:5b

If you are in pain right now, it may be because something new is about to happen. Pain always precedes progress. When you hold that precious new baby in your arms, the pain of the labor will melt into the joy of the new birth. When you feel the pain, it is not the time to give up; rather, it is the time to anticipate the blessings that are coming. "Weeping may last through the night, but joy comes with the morning" (Ps. 30:5). Pain is gain.

Hosea 6:1–3 says:

> "Come, let us return to the LORD. He has torn us to pieces; now He will heal us. He has injured us; now He will bandage our wounds. In just a short time He will restore us, so that we may live in His presence. Oh, that we might know the LORD! Let us press on to know Him. He will respond to us as surely as the arrival of the dawn or the coming of rains in early spring."

Paul says the same thing in Romans 8:22–23:

> For we all know that all creation has been groaning as in the pains of childbirth right up to the present time. And we believers also groan, even though we have the

Holy Spirit within us as a foretaste of future glory, for we long for our bodies to be released from sin and suffering. We, too, wait with eager hope for the day when God will give us our full rights as His adopted children, including the new bodies He has promised us.

When you are hurting, can you remember that your pain is a reminder of God's promise? The hurt means the healing is on the way. The prophet Isaiah said, "For I am about to do something new. See, I have already begun! Do you not see it? I will make a pathway through the wilderness. I will create rivers in the dry wasteland" (Isa. 43:19). Right now, your wilderness and your wastelands are in the process of being turned into roads and rivers. It has already begun. Just because something has not arrived does not mean it is not coming. Whether it's a season of joy that's just around the bend or finally fulfilled on the other side of glory, your pain is leading to your pathway.

"It's not over yet. He'll turn every heartache to a hallelujah. He'll turn every tear to a pearl. He'll turn every sunset to a sunrise. And He'll turn every Calvary to an Easter."
Adrian Rogers

Day 34

No First Amendment Rights with God

Even fools are thought wise when they keep silent.
Proverbs 17:28a

As a believer, you have lost your First Amendment right to free speech. You don't have the right to say something just because you feel like it. You don't have the right to say something cruel because it will get a laugh. You don't even have the right to say something simply because it is true. Every word that comes out of your mouth must first pass two tests. Will what you say bring glory and honor to Christ? Is it a word that will build up and edify those who hear it?

If not, then it is a word that should remain unsaid. The wisest people say the least. The godliest people get the fewest low-jab laughs. I have told you that what I write about isn't always what I have mastered. Far too many times my wit has trumped my wisdom.

It is better to be considered slow and dull than to be considered quick and cruel. Actually, you might not be so quick-witted if you actually took time to think before you speak. And that's a good thing. Your words need time to pass through a filter before they exit your mouth. No one loves a quick and timely wisecrack more than me. I tell people I know I am intelligent because all my life I've been told that I have a "smart" mouth. Unfortunately, God values slowness. James 1:19 commands us to be "slow to speak." God wants you to think before you speak.

Someone put together this acrostic for THINK:

T: Is it TRUE?
H: Is it HELPFUL?
I: Is it INSPIRING?
N: Is it NECESSARY?
K: Is it KIND?

It has been said, "A smart person knows what to say. A wise person knows whether or not to say it."

*"Many things are opened by mistake but
none so frequently as the mouth."*
Adrian Rogers

Day 35

Sometimes You Just Need to Climb a Tree

He tried to get a look at Jesus, but he was too short to see over the crowd. So he ran ahead and climbed a sycamore-fig tree beside the road, for Jesus was going to pass that way.
Luke 19:3–4

One of my favorite Bible stories is about a "wee little man" named Zacchaeus. This little man was more than simply curious. He didn't just suffer from FOMO (fear of missing out). He didn't want to see *what*. He wanted to see *who*. He wanted to see Jesus. He may have been a hated tax collector, but that isn't what he was remembered for. He couldn't see because he was too short and the crowd was too tall. He had obstacles that seemed impossible. I love what happened next. He made it happen. He was strategic. He was determined. There is nothing wrong with combining your faith with your brain. God gave you both.

Luke says that instead of giving up and giving in, he ran ahead and climbed up into a tree. I hope you can see the significance of that. When you have an opportunity of life-changing importance like seeing Jesus, don't just say, "Oh well. Too bad, so sad. Why am I short?" Be like Zacchaeus. He thought through what it would take to make it happen, and he proactively and strategically changed his circumstances. He didn't stay where he was and fret. He ran ahead to make preparations. He looked to see what he *did* have that he could use. And there it was, a sycamore tree.

Zacchaeus couldn't change his height. He couldn't change the crowd. But he could change his vantage point. He did what w*as* in his power to do. And guess what? When Jesus passed through, he not only saw Jesus, but Jesus saw him. Out of all the people in the crowds, this "wee little man" was the one to whom Jesus said, "Hurry and come down out of that tree, for today I must stay at your house" (see v. 5). When he did his part, Zacchaeus got far more than just a glimpse. He got Jesus all to himself!

Are you simply resigning yourself to the current outcome because anything else seems impossible? Sometimes waiting is the right thing to do. Other times, running ahead and climbing a tree is the right action. Whichever one you are led to do, just make sure your goal is to see Jesus. When it is, He will see you, too.

"If you have faith like Zacchaeus,
Jesus will go home with you, too."
Adrian Rogers

Day 36

It Won't Cost Anything but Time

*But God showed His great love for us by sending
Christ to die for us while we were still sinners.*
Romans 5:8

To make someone feel something, you must take the time to connect beneath the surface level. Without this, it is impossible to show genuine respect and add true value.

This isn't a "drive-by" connection. You have to slow down. Actually, you have to stop. To get to this level, the connection can't be superficial. You can't rehearse small talk or spout platitudes. It has been said, "If you can fake sincerity, you have it made." That's because you *can't* fake sincerity. At least, not for long. Genuine connection reaches below the waterline into the deepest parts of another soul. If it is genuine, it will eventually hit its mark.

Many times you will know when your words have gone deep enough to touch another's soul because tears will form in their eyes. These may be tears because you have touched something that hurts, but they aren't tears of hurt. When you care enough to go beneath the surface, you let a person know that you care about who they really are, not the mask they wear. Genuine care travels both ways through tears. Never be ashamed of them.

You must realize, however, that if you recoil in judgment at what you find, you will never get the chance again. You can only pour in the healing balm of kindness when you tenderly open up buried memories of old wounds in a spirit of acceptance. Only then can you gently prove that you value the real person they are beneath their mask. Genuine love never allows what someone has done to define who they are.

Most people believe that if you *really* knew them, you couldn't love them. Only when you tenderly probe their soul, acknowledge their pain, and affirm them regardless of what you find, will they feel safe. When they feel safe, because of your acceptance, they will open themselves up to the grace of God that you can then lavishly administer.

Take the time to truly know someone. If you don't know who someone is, how can you genuinely value anything more than their persona? Even they know their persona is fake. Acceptance of that persona has no true worth. Surface kindness is better than rudeness, but it has no lasting benefit. "Beneath-the-surface kindness" is the most valuable gift you can give another human being, and it costs nothing.

*"No one has ever sinned themselves
beyond the love of God."*
Adrian Rogers

Day 37

Your Emotional Warning Light Is On

Before Abraham was even born, I AM!
John 8:58b

In the same way the check-engine light warns you on the dashboard of your car, bad feelings are a signal from God that something is wrong. When you feel unloved, don't go "looking for love in all the wrong places." No, it is a cue from God that you need to find your love in Him. When the warning light goes on, always consult the manual. Jeremiah 31:3 says, "I have loved you, my people, with an everlasting love."

When you feel lonely, don't throw a pity party for yourself. That feeling is a cue that you are not finding your companionship in Jesus. Check your manual. Hebrews 13:5b says, "I will never fail you. I will never abandon you." God has not left you.

When you feel rejected, you need to be the one doing the rejecting. You need to reject that feeling because it is a lie from Satan. Your emotional warning light is telling you to check your manual. God's Word says in Ephesians 1:6 (NKJV): "to the praise of the glory of His grace, by which He made us accepted in the Beloved."

When you feel afraid, it is a warning signal, a cue, that you have forgotten who God is: "The LORD is my light and my salvation—so why should I be afraid?" (Ps. 27:1a).

When you are worried, it is a sign you are carrying your own burdens. First Peter 5:7 says, "Give all your worries and cares to God, for He cares about you."

What if I haven't named your need? Jesus covered it all when He said in John 8:58b, "Before Abraham was even born, I AM!" The incompleteness of that sentence is an invitation for you to fill in the blank. Whatever you need, Jesus is!

There is a rare and dangerous disease named CIPA (congenital insensitivity to pain with anhidrosis) that makes a person unable to feel pain. When you don't hurt, you don't know when you need help. Thank God for negative emotions. They should serve to let you know to check your manual!

"You must master your emotions, or your emotions will master you."
Adrian Rogers

Day 38

The Top Five Things You Need to Do Every Day

Train yourself to be godly.
1 Timothy 4:7b

There are many things you need to do every day. Here are the top five:

1. Have a daily devotional routine. The first thing you should do is put on the full armor of God. Don't do anything unprotected. Then read God's Word. Have a plan. Pick out part of that passage to be memorizing and meditating on throughout the day. Complete your morning routine with prayer. Begin with praise and thanksgiving. Prayer should always begin with His glory, not your wish list. Continue your prayer time with confession of your sins and asking for His fresh infilling and anointing. Finish with intercession for others and personal requests for yourself.

2. Always be reading one or two great books about Christian living. Wholesome fiction is fine for entertainment, but it doesn't cut it for spiritual growth. Mark your books up, star your favorite passages, make them yours. If you haven't written all over them and underlined meaningful sentences, they aren't really yours. Every book should be *"red."* Own your books. Make them your friends!

3. Proactively plan your calendar by scheduling time with family and loved ones. In addition, intentionally schedule time with spiritually

mature friends who will give you wise counsel and partner with you in prayer. Do this before other activities.

4. View each encounter throughout the day, whether by phone, text, or in person, as a divine appointment. Give a smile, an encouraging word, a dose of hope. Do an act of selfless kindness each day. God intends for you to pass on everything He puts into you.

5. Faithfully perform whatever your work may be in a methodical, organized way. Do the tasks you are responsible for day in and day out, as unto the Lord and not unto men. Be disciplined with your time. Plan your day in advance, but always create margin for God to work, lead, and redirect. Budget your money. Live on a cash basis. Don't buy things you do not need with money you do not have. Be generous to others before you are indulgent with yourself. Finally, take care of your health. You are a steward of what you do to your body.

There are more, but you'll do well starting with this checklist. You are responsible for the actions; God is responsible for the results. Eric Thomas said, "Fall in love with the process and the results will come."[6]

"Discipline says, 'I need to.' Duty says, 'I ought to.' Devotion says, 'I want to.'"
Adrian Rogers

Day 39

Are You on the Verge of Giving Up?

*The faithful love of the L*ORD *never ends! His mercies never cease.*
Great is His faithfulness; His mercies begin afresh each morning.
Lamentations 3:22–23

Has the same sin defeated you time and time again? Do you feel that each time you allow your head to cautiously pop up out of the ground, the devil takes a hammer and bashes you right back down? It's almost like an arcade game of Whac-A-Mole. My granddaughter asks me to build architectural masterpieces for her out of Play-Doh. The instant I proudly complete one, she says, "Squish!" and slams her hand on top of it. That's what I feel Satan does to me when I make any type of spiritual progress.

The good news is that no matter how many times you have failed, there is still mercy, forgiveness, and hope.

God won't ever give up on you. Satan wants you to think you've run out of chances. He wants you to give in and give up. He wants to shame, humiliate, and weigh you down with unbearable guilt. He wants to take his fingers and snuff out your last little flickering flame of hope. But praise God, the faithful love of God never ends. Second Timothy 2:13 says, "If we are unfaithful, He remains faithful, for He cannot deny who He is." It isn't about who you are or what you have done. It is about who He is and what He has done!

The fact that you've been focusing on who you are is the entire problem in the first place. You feel guilty because of your failures and inadequacies, so you try to overcome your sinfulness by willpower and increased effort. You never will. Actually, you can't. Your only option is to give up and allow God to do it through you. Fact number one: you can't win. But hallelujah for fact number two: He has already won. If Satan can keep your focus on you and your failure, you will not tap into the victory that is already yours. He knows that if he can keep you looking back at your sin, you will not be able to look toward your Savior.

You don't win by intensifying your efforts. It is quite the opposite. Just empty yourself. All you need to do is allow His power to flow unhindered through your emptiness. Confess your sins. Confess your inadequacies. And then let it flow. You don't provide the power; your confession and repentance empty the vessel through which the power flows.

"God doesn't want me to do anything for Him.
He wants to do something through me."
Adrian Rogers

Day 40

You Are the GOAT at Being You

*In His grace, God has given us different gifts
for doing certain things well.*
Romans 12:6

You are not a faceless and insignificant number among the billions and billions of people who have ever lived. You are a timeless masterpiece, created with a special purpose, for a specific reason. He created you with something unique in mind. There is no one else exactly like you in the entire universe. Scarcity is what determines value. When you try to fit in, you neutralize your value. Try to stand out.

God has "good works" for you to perform that need your special touch. Your giftings could be the only key that will open certain locks. If you did not exist, there would be a huge void. That means you better not be piddling away your time with meaningless and trivial entertainment. A magnet on my refrigerator says: "I could do great things if I were not so busy doing little things." God has gifted you in certain areas that you do well because He has something in mind that will require those skills. If you are doing something that does not require those skills, then I suspect you are not doing the thing for which you were created.

Many times Satan will tell you that you are not good in the areas that are actually your strengths. That is a genius strategy. Because of your perfectionistic tendencies, you may be particularly susceptible in the areas of your proficiencies. Don't fall for this. Satan is trying to neutralize your greatest potential impact for the kingdom.

Romans 12:6b says, "In His grace, God has given us different gifts for doing certain things well." Yes! That means you! God has gifted you. Poor-mouthing yourself is not being humble. It is failing to honor your Creator. God has equipped you. God will empower you. Be mighty in the areas of your giftings. Develop them. Cherish them. Use them.

"God has a purpose and a plan for me that no one else can fulfill."
Adrian Rogers

Day 41

Complete in Christ

So you also are complete through your union with Christ.
Colossians 2:10

If you could only realize the meaning of the little phrase found in Colossians 2:10, it would change your life! The phrase is "So you also are complete." You can think of any relationship, but for the sake of illustration, I want you to think of your relationship with your spouse. Because you are "one flesh" with him, does that mean he is supposed to be the one to complete you by meeting all of your needs? Absolutely not! Your spouse was never intended to occupy the place of God. That's a recipe for disaster. Instead, when you are complete in Christ, you will find that is what allows you to selflessly pour yourself into your husband. Only a complete person can give 100 percent. Think about that statement.

When you don't depend on your spouse to make you whole, you are free! You are free to enjoy each other. You are free to give of yourself, even when he has nothing to give back. You are free to love him with God's agape love, which is a giving love, rather than a taking love. When you need your spouse to complete you, it isn't possible to have that type of love. You are always desperate to get what you must have. He is also desperate to get what he must have. It has the makings of a good divorce. At the very least, it has the makings of a lifelong battle. Sooner, rather than later, you are both going to let each other down.

If that is where you find yourself, let me ask what happened. The problem wasn't on God's end. The problem was that you gave each other a place that only belonged to God. Your husband is an imperfect sinner (I'm sure you've already figured that out). It was only a matter of time before it was discovered. And I am equally sure that when it was discovered, the emotional hurt was greater than any emotional emptiness you felt before you were married. This is because the deeper the relationship, the greater the hurt. You are hurt because you and I are created to be complete in Christ alone. When you allow Christ to complete you, you will realize that He will give you enough love to overflow that love unconditionally into an undeserving spouse.

Letting Christ complete you is the only thing that allows you to open yourself up to someone else in a vulnerable way. Until Christ is your everything, you are not able to take risks in love. You can take risks because you don't have to be self-protective. That human person you love no longer has the ability to destroy you. You are finally able to give and give. When you do that, I imagine he will become motivated to give back. Even if it doesn't happen that way, you will still be perfectly complete. It's a no-lose proposition.

"I have never known a time when
God was not totally sufficient."
Adrian Rogers

Day 42

Is God Enough?

*You adulterers! Don't you realize that friendship
with the world makes you an enemy of God?*
James 4:4a

I don't want pleasures, positions, power, or possessions. Even the "good" things I have sought in prayer become evil things when they serve to replace the Giver of the gifts. It is so wrong to fill the emptiness of my soul with this world's passions and pursuits. Why would God give me things that would silence my soul's desperation for Him? Satan has deceived me into thinking that presenting my wish list of personal comforts qualifies me for fulfilling God's commandment to pray.

The impact of that is life-altering. Friendship with the things of this world, regardless of how innocent those things may be, is warfare with God. First John 2:15–16 clearly states:

> Do not love this world nor the things it offers you, for when you love the world, you do not have the love of the Father in you. For the world offers only a craving for physical pleasure, a craving for everything we see, and pride in our achievements and possessions. They are not from the Father, but are from this world.

God would no more answer your requests for the things you desire to replace Him than you would purchase gift cards for your husband to take another woman out to dinner. James 4:2b–4 strongly says:

> Yet you don't have what you want because you don't ask God for it. And even when you ask, you don't get it because your motives are all wrong—you only want what will give you pleasure. You adulterers! Don't you realize that friendship with the world makes you an enemy of God? I say it again: If you want to be a friend of the world, you make yourself an enemy of God.

Steve Marcum (my life group leader) once asked this sobering question to our group: "If God were to answer all your prayers with a yes, how many people would be impacted for the kingdom of God?" Ask yourself that question. Is God Himself enough for you, or is He just your genie? Is He nothing more than a magical person who grants your wishes and serves your purposes when you call Him?

"There are too many spiritual forgers signing Jesus's name to their prayer checks."
Adrian Rogers

Day 43

Tears in a Bottle and Hairs on Your Head

You keep track of all my sorrows. You have collected all my tears in Your bottle. You have recorded each one in Your book.
Psalm 56:8

There is no more tender, compassionate fact than that the God who created the universe cares about every tear you have ever cried. This isn't just a general thought expressing that God is a God of compassion. It is even more staggering than that. Almighty God keeps track of, collects, and records every tear *you* shed in *His* bottle (not just a generic bottle but *His* bottle) with *your* name on it. When you think you are weeping alone in the night, you are not alone. There is no tear that He does not share. If you have a hard time memorizing Scripture, you can memorize this one, "Jesus wept" (John 11:35). He is the God who sees. He is the God who cares. He is the God who remembers.

Not only does this God see and collect every tear you shed, but He also numbers every hair on your head. "What is the price of five sparrows—two copper coins? Yet God does not forget a single one of them. And the very hairs on your head are all numbered. So don't be afraid; you are more valuable to God than a whole flock of sparrows" (Luke 12:6–7).

There is nothing concerning you that does not concern Him. "The LORD directs the steps of the godly. He delights in every detail of their lives" (Ps. 37:23). Oh, dear friend, I pray that the eyes of your heart would be enlightened so that you can see the unfathomable love of the Father. Every tear, every hair, every detail!

In Psalm 139:1–4 David says, "O Lord, you have examined my heart and know everything about me. You know when I sit down or stand up. You know my thoughts even when I'm far away. You see me when I travel and when I rest at home. You know everything I do. You know what I am going to say even before I say it, Lord." Then He says, "How precious are your thoughts about me, O God. They cannot be numbered! I can't even count them; they outnumber the grains of sand! And when I wake up, You are still with me!" (Ps. 139:17–18). When you finish memorizing, "Jesus wept," I think the entirety of Psalm 139 would be a life-altering text to attempt next.

Frederick Lehman penned these words in 1917: "Could we with ink the ocean fill, and were the skies of parchment made; Were every stalk on earth a quill, and every man a scribe by trade; to write the love of God above would drain the ocean dry; nor could the scroll contain the whole, though stretched from sky to sky."[7]

> *"God is going to turn every tear into a pearl and string them for a diadem for you."*
> **Adrian Rogers**

Day 44

True Love

There is no greater love than to lay down one's life for one's friends.
John 15:13

Here's a big announcement: being "in love" has absolutely nothing to do with true love. Being in love is probably the most fleeting feeling on earth. I'm going to let you in on a secret. When Mike and I got married, we wrote our own vows. I was expecting Mike to say in his vows that he was in love with me. I know he was, but he didn't write that in his vows. Instead, he wrote: "I commit to love you as an act of my will." I confess, that even in the wedding ceremony, I was a little put off by that. I wanted to hear about his "feelings." But as the years have come and gone, oh, how grateful I am that Mike has loved me as an act of his will. We wouldn't be married today if he had not.

In English, we use the same word to describe our feelings for hot dogs that we use to describe our feelings for our mates. But the Greeks had four different words for love:

- *Eros:* A romantic love involving sexual attraction
- *Phileo:* An affectionate friendship love
- S*torge:* A deep longing between family members
- *Agape:* God's love that always does the right thing

Agape love has nothing whatsoever to do with feelings. Agape love is an action based on doing what is best for someone else, regardless of whether you even like the person you "agape." Over the years I am sure there have been thousands of times Mike has thought, *I love you, but right now there is nothing about you that I even remotely like.*

Agape is the word used for love in 1 Corinthians 13: "Love is patient and kind. Love is not jealous or boastful or proud or rude. It does not demand its own way. It is not irritable, and it keeps no record of being wronged" (vv. 4–5). Being "in love" is not what keeps couples together. Practicing agape love when your spouse is unlovable is what keeps you together.

"When you operate with agape love, you make a choice apart from emotion or feeling."
Adrian Rogers

Day 45

How to Become Obedient

*My old self has been crucified with Christ. It is no
longer I who live, but Christ lives in me.*
Galatians 2:20

I'm not a compliant person. Too many times obedience represents defeat to me. I want to win, even when I am wrong. Like a horse, I'm not usable until I am meeked. Obedience should not be a fight to the death. I heard that obedience should be viewed as an invitation. It is an invitation to follow Christ.

Ask God to give you the gift of a submissive spirit. Why do we all hate the word *submission*? We are afraid of being taken advantage of. But God wants you to be submissive to your husband in order to bless you. To not want a submissive spirit is to be afraid of God's goodness. When you get your way, you don't get God's way. Whose way is better?

Voluntarily take on the role of a servant. Jesus "gave up His divine privileges; He took the humble position of a slave" (Phil. 2:7). Though He was God, Jesus let go of the rights of Godhood, and He embraced servanthood. When meeting another's needs becomes your utmost desire, there will be no drudgery in submission. A true servant only finds pleasure in pleasing her master.

Resolutely decide to be uncompromisingly obedient. Jesus knew in advance that becoming a man would involve dying a cruel death. He came anyway. You, too, must decide in advance that you will obey regardless of the cost. This is a daily decision. Paul said in 1 Corinthians

15:31, "I die daily" (NASB). Each time you do, you will experience more grace.

Each morning I stretch out my arms in the shape of a cross. I say, "I am dead to my own desires. I am dead to my own plans. I am dead to my rights. I am dead to my opinions. My old self has been crucified with You, Jesus. It is no longer I who lives, but You who live in me. Because I have entered into Your death, I am raised along with You. I am raised to do what You desire me to do. I am raised to follow Your plans for my day. I am raised to glorify You. It doesn't matter what anyone does to offend or take advantage of me today. Who can offend or take advantage of a dead man?"

I challenge you to do this exercise before you even get out of bed in the morning. Next, put on the full armor of God. Then, fill up with God's Word. You will be ready for the day!

"He died to claim me as Lord. He lives to control me as Lord."
Adrian Rogers

Day 46

A Lost Phone

*As the deer longs for streams of water, so I long for
You, O God. I thirst for God, the living God.*
Psalm 42:1–2

I have lost my cell phone several times. One time it was gone for an entire week. I will say parenthetically that I'm not certain this book would exist if my phone had been with me that week. Without my phone, God was able to speak clearly to me.

In addition to being able to focus on God without distraction, I realized there was a restlessness inside of me that felt like a part of me I couldn't live without was cut off. Obviously, there is a problem in that area of my life.

Here is the part that is convicting to me, and I want to ask if it is convicting to you. How many days have you gone throughout the entire day without spending time in God's Word? How many days has God's Word not been at the forefront of your mind? Meditation is simply reflecting back on the Scripture God gave you in the morning as often as you would check your phone for text messages or your Facebook for updates. If you can live without God's Word abiding in your heart during the day, but you can't live without your cell phone attached to your hip, something is desperately wrong with where you are drawing your strength.

Do you long for God's Word the way you long for your lost phone? Isaiah 26:9a, "All night long I search for You; in the morning I earnestly seek for God." Psalm 63:1 says: "O God, You are my God; I earnestly search for You. My soul thirsts for You; my whole body longs for You in this parched and weary land where there is no water." Psalm 119:35–37, "Make me walk along the path of Your commands, for that is where my happiness is found. Give me an eagerness for Your laws rather than a love for money! Turn my eyes from worthless things, and give me life through Your word." Psalm 119:147–148 says, "I rise early, before the sun is up; I cry out for help and put my hope in Your words. I stay awake through the night, thinking about Your promise." The Scriptures are filled with verses like these. These are just the tip of the iceberg.

How ashamed I am that being unable to hourly check my phone (or my social media feed) made me so out of sorts. God uses things like a lost phone to make us realize how far we have to go in our spiritual journey.

> *"The Word of God is to your spirit what blood is to your body."*
> **Adrian Rogers**

Day 47

It Is Time!

Unseal my lips, O Lord, that my mouth may praise You.
Psalm 51:15

Many reading these words think they have forfeited God's calling in their lives because of their previous moral failure. If this is you, I want you to pay careful attention. One of Satan's chief strategies is to shut your lips and silence your testimony. He fears your victory over your moral failings will give hope to the prisoners he is currently holding captive. He is holding them captive with imaginary prison bars created in their own minds by believing his lie that they can never again be made clean. Your victory exposes his lie. That is a threat!

For obvious reasons, Satan desires to make you believe that your sin disqualifies you from being a spokesperson for Christ. He needs to silence your testimony of grace, and once again, the only tool he has to do that with is another lie. In reality, your sin is the only thing that qualifies you to be a recipient of grace. Think about that. The greater your sin, the greater your testimony of deliverance! The greater your sin, the greater your message of hope. The greater your sin, the greater witness you have of the unfathomable depth and width and height of His limitless grace. Seriously. Think about that.

Yes, you may have grievously sinned. But look at the hope found in Psalm 51. King David committed adultery and covered it up with murder. And yet, he is the one God chose to pen the majority of the psalms that fill our hearts with hope. Satan, not God, is the one who will tell you that if you have sinned grievously God is finished with you. Satan is the one who will tell you that God has cast you off. It is a lie! There is nothing you can ever do that will make God stop loving you. Nothing! But you do need to repent. And repentance means not only to confess but to turn and go in the opposite direction.

If you have truly repented, your sins have been completely forgiven, regardless of what they were. Psalm 51:1 says that even the stain of your sin will be blotted out. Something clean may still be unusable because of the stain. But true repentance washes out both the guilt and the stain. That is cause for a hallelujah! And that is what I want you to notice. This great sinner, David, said in Psalm 51:2, "Wash me clean from my guilt. Purify me from my sin." Then in Psalm 51:13, he said, "Then I will teach Your ways to rebels, and they will return to You." In Psalm 51:15 David said again, "Unseal my lips, O Lord, that my mouth may praise You." David, the murderer and the adulterer, repented and asked God to unseal his lips. You need to unseal yours. It is time! Only sinners can testify of grace.

"For great sin, there is great grace!"
Adrian Rogers

Day 48

How to Love People You Don't Like

*Most important of all, continue to show deep love for
each other, for love covers a multitude of sins.*
1 Peter 4:8

When you don't like someone, do you find joy in pointing out areas of hypocrisy and inconsistency in their life? Or do you delight in shining the spotlight on the good and praiseworthy? When you dig, are you looking for dirt or gold? Basically, do you love others the same way Christ loves you?

Let me make it even more personal. Visualize the specific person you don't like. Do you give her (or him) the same grace Christ gives you? Do you cover her offenses with the blood of Christ the way He has covered your offenses through His blood? I am not talking about enabling someone's poor choices or justifying their sin. I'm talking about forgiveness and grace. Do you carry them before the throne in prayer or throw them under the bus in gossip?

I have a long way to go, but when I am around someone I don't care for, I ask God to enable me to look at them through His eyes. Instead of hoping they will just go away, I now ask Jesus what He desires to do in them. He created them like they are for a reason. If they were restored to the original plan He had in mind for them, what would that look like? I think about what He has done for me and try to visualize what they could be if they were to allow Him to do the same thing for them.

I know I am different because of His grace. If I have changed, why couldn't He do the same for them?

I don't stop there. I then ask God to show them His love through me. I no longer hide when I see them coming or hope they won't be invited to the events I attend. I know that everyone will not become my best friend, but I also know that biblical love isn't about emotion. It is about action. Agape love (the Greek word for Godlike, sacrificial love) doesn't involve feelings at all. It is doing the right thing because it is the right thing, even at great cost to yourself. Sometimes you come to love those people you don't like. Other times, you show love to people you will never enjoy. Either way, it's still agape love. Ask God to change you first, then be available to be the one to show His love to them. It will do as much for you as it will for them.

"Forgiveness is not an emotion; it's a choice."
Adrian Rogers

Day 49

What If God Is Giving You a Second Chance?

Give us gladness in proportion to our former misery! Replace the evil years with good.
Psalm 90:15

Are you experiencing any type of loss right now? What if you consider this loss as a blessing? What if it is an opportunity to begin again? Have you lost your job? Your home? Your credit score? Your marriage? Your best friend? Your reputation? It could be that God has allowed the rubble to be cleared away in order to get down to the foundation. He may want to begin a *new* work. Wouldn't you love to start over? Wouldn't you love to have a second chance? Maybe what you have been interpreting as a disaster is God's way of saying, "Hey, let's start fresh. This time let Me take the lead."

Can you remember when you had a dream? Maybe there was something you always felt God wanted you to do, but the day-to-day affairs of life kept you so busy and weighed down that you never pursued it. What if God, in His wisdom and love, took away what kept you so busy? You have two options. You could go into a paralyzing depression, or you could use the newfound free time to devote your energy to your dream. It's all in how you frame it. Maybe, just maybe, instead of God harming you, He is giving you an opportunity. Step outside your comfort zone and do something outrageously different. It could be that you haven't had time to do something extraordinary because you were so busy being ordinary. He is giving you an opportunity that is even bigger than *doing* something different. Maybe He is giving you an opportunity to *be* somebody different.

Have you lost your job? Start your own business. Go back to school and finish your degree. Write your book. Disciple your grandchildren. Don't die with what God wants you to do still inside you. When God takes something away, look at it as the opportunity to do something new. Thank God that He forced you to make a change you didn't have enough courage to make on your own. He is making space for what is about to come. Rock bottom is a solid foundation on which to rebuild your life.

"Our God is a God of second chances."
Adrian Rogers

Day 50

Standing at the Crossroads

This is what the LORD says: "Stop at the crossroads and look around. Ask for the old, godly way, and walk in it. Travel its path, and you will find rest for your souls." But you reply, "No, that's not the road we want!"
Jeremiah 6:16

Today sin is not only tolerated; it's celebrated. I don't care what kind of sin it is, when you strike up the band and throw a parade, you kindle the wrath of a holy God. Ephesians 5:12 says, "It is shameful even to talk about the things that ungodly people do in secret." Yet it seems everywhere we look—whether its media, education, or Hollywood—our society finds ways to applaud those who embody all types of sin. Jesus Himself said in red letters in Matthew 18:6, "But if you cause one of these little ones who trusts in Me to fall into sin, it would be better for you to have a large millstone tied around your neck and be drowned in the depths of the sea."

To speak any sort of truth, or simply believe biblical principles, in today's atmosphere is often interpreted as hatred. But is it hateful to teach an entire generation to choose evil? Is it hateful to warn people what will happen if they do? People didn't want to hear the truth Jesus spoke. It got Him crucified. People won't want to hear it from you, either. They will symbolically crucify you, as well. Adrian Rogers said, "It is better to be hated for telling the truth than loved for telling a lie."

Our nation—and so many of the Christians within it—are at a crossroads. Be careful which path you choose. They end in two completely different places. Jesus said in Matthew 7:13–14: "You can enter God's Kingdom only through the narrow gate. The highway to hell is broad, and its gate is wide for the many who choose that way. But the gateway to life is very narrow and the road is difficult, and only a few ever find it."

Do you feel that you are the only one left who stands for the truth? Walk in the "old, godly way . . . and you will find rest for your souls" (Jer. 6:16).

"Sin that used to slink down the back alley now struts down the main street."
Adrian Rogers

Day 51

Dying with Grace because of Dying Grace

*I prayed to the L*ORD*, and he answered me. He freed me from all my fears. Those who look to Him for help will be radiant with joy.*
Psalm 34:4–5a

My friend Whitney was a young mom with three little boys, and she was dying of an incurable cancer. When Whitney's friends went to minister to her, they didn't find a person who was hopeless and miserable. Astonishingly, they found a person full of life, living each day with sheer, unbridled joy. Yes, she was weak, but she was radiant. The person being ministered to became the person doing the ministering. And Whitney's joy wasn't because God was delivering her from death. It was because He was walking through the valley of death *with* her. He was giving her "dying grace."

Whitney died on February 27, 2020. But did she? No, Whitney didn't die. She graduated to glory. With honors, I might add. She wasn't being punished; she was receiving her reward. And in the midst of pain and suffering, she kept a smile on her face and an encouraging word for everyone who came to visit. Her heart never ached for herself, only for her precious children and the family she left behind.

Whitney showed us how to live as well as how to die. In the midst of her pain, she passed from this life into the next, sustained by God's grace and continually filled with His peace that "passes all understanding" (RSV). His peace held her fast until the end. Whitney didn't want you to cry for her. Instead, she wanted to encourage you. When you came to comfort her, she would draw you close and say with a radiant smile, "Come, let us tell of the LORD's greatness; let us exalt His name together" (Ps. 34:3).

I know many of you have been through deep sorrow and unfathomable pain. Are you receiving the grace God makes available to you? It's there in such great proportions that even in your darkest hour there will still be enough left for you to pass along to others.

"We spend more time in our prayer meetings trying to keep the saints out of heaven than the sinners of out hell."
Adrian Rogers

Day 52

Are You Waiting on God, or Is God Waiting on You?

So the LORD must wait for you to come to Him so He can show you His love and compassion. For the LORD is a faithful God. Blessed are those who wait for His help.
Isaiah 30:18

Nothing is harder than to wait. But remember, the fancier the dinner, the longer the prep time. You can fill up on crackers if you want, but you won't be hungry when the feast is ready. No one is stopping you. You're only hurting yourself. Charles Stanley said, "You can wait on God or wish you had."[8]

For a long time, I felt like my life was at a standstill. I would pray and hear nothing. I would ask for direction and receive silence. I desperately needed money, and there was nothing to deposit. I finally said yes in an area where I had been disobedient, and the answers started to flow. It wasn't God causing the delay. It was me.

One of my favorite poems was written in 1890 by Francis Thompson. It epically tells the story of a man frantically running from God, "The Hound of Heaven." This desperate man was fleeing from the person who was tracking him down in order to bless him. The classic poem begins, "I fled Him, down the nights and down the days; I fled Him, down the arches of the years." It concludes with the heavenly Hound coming to the end of His lifelong pursuit and saying, "All which I took from thee I did but take, not for thy harms, but just that thou might'st seek it in My arms. All which thy child's mistake fancies as lost, I have stored for thee at home: Rise, clasp My hand, come!" Read that a dozen times if you must in order to get it. It's profound.

Sometimes you are irritated when you should be grateful. God is preparing a special feast. Just wait for it. It will be worth it. Other times it is God who is waiting on you. He is waiting for you to quit running and say yes to what He has long ago asked you to do. Are you finally ready? God has been waiting to bless you for a long time.

The disciples frantically fished all night without a single catch. Jesus patiently watched them from the shore, waiting on them to finally give up and look to Him. When at last they did, there were "more fish than their nets could hold" (see John 21:6). There are times when you *do* need to wait on God, but whatever you do, don't keep the God of the universe waiting on you.

> *"Waiting on the Lord is like waiting for the sun to come up. You can't hurry it. You can't stop it. God is going to bring a sunrise to your soul. Just wait for it and trust Him while you wait."*
> **Adrian Rogers**

Day 53

Drinks Are on the House!

"Is anyone thirsty? Come and drink—even if you have no money! Come, take your choice of wine or milk—it's all free!"
Isaiah 55:1

You can have anything you want! It's your choice and it's all free! If you are flat broke, this is the invitation you've been waiting for. It is far more exciting than little impoverished Charlie opening that golden ticket and gaining admittance to Willy Wonka's Chocolate Factory. It sounds too good to be true, but the One who owns it all has selected the finest and has offered it to you in unlimited portions. The apostle Paul repeats this same promise in Ephesians 1:3 when he says, "All praise to God, the Father of our Lord Jesus Christ, who has blessed us with every spiritual blessing in the heavenly realms because we are united with Christ." The finest of everything is all free.

The big question is: Why would you eat off the dollar menu when the most nutritious and delicious food and drink have been lavishly offered to you? Isaiah goes on to say, "Why spend your money on food that does not give you strength? Why pay for food that does you no good? Listen to Me, and you will eat what is good. You will enjoy the finest food" (Isa. 55:2).

So the question is: *Why?* Why are you dumpster diving? Why are you seeking satisfaction in the pitiful substitutes your pocket change can buy? Do you really think money and the temporal things money can buy are the answer? Never equate money and things with God's blessing. Even if you have enough money to buy everything you want, you will still want the wrong things. You will always make the poor choices. Even if you buy it all, you will still come up empty. Haggai 1:6 says, "You have planted much but harvest little. You eat but are not satisfied. You drink but are still thirsty. You put on clothes but cannot keep warm. Your wages disappear as though you were putting them in pockets filled with holes!" Only Jesus can satisfy. And He does it freely and fully. Come and drink deeply from the fountain of spiritual abundance. Eat and drink to your heart's content! It sounds too good to be true, but it isn't!

> *"You'll see how rich you are when you add up everything you have that money can't buy and death can't take away."*
> **Adrian Rogers**

Day 54

Relational Stewardship

As iron sharpens iron, so a friend sharpens a friend.
Proverbs 27:17

Webster's dictionary describes a steward as "someone who manages the property of another." The most obvious application of that is in the area of your finances. But biblical stewardship extends to relationships. People are also on loan to you by God. Colossians 1:25 (ESV) says, "I became a minister according to the stewardship from God that was given to me for you."

God is never content when you simply maintain anything He has given to you. He wants you to multiply His assets. In the parable of the talents in Matthew 25:14–21, the master returned to receive an account of what the three stewards had done to increase his investment during his absence. The steward who was only given one talent took the one talent he was given and buried it in the ground. It is so interesting that he didn't squander what he had been given. He didn't lose it. It wasn't diminished in value. But when the master returned, the master was still angry that the steward had not, at least, invested it in some way that would have caused it to grow.

Stewardship in the area of finances is obvious, but actually, stewardship with your relationships is the most important form of stewardship. The more valuable the possession, the more serious the offense of not producing a positive return on that possession.

In the book *The Blessing*, Gary Smalley said that all children are given to parents filled only with potential. Smalley said parents have a role to play when it comes to that potential. God didn't give children to parents to make the parents happy. He gave children to parents so that those parents could develop the potential God put into the children. Whether you are a parent or not, the same is true in every close relationship God has given to you. Your job is always to enrich lives. Your job is to build up. Your job is to replenish. You should always see what you can pour into someone and never what you can get out of them. Relational stewardship means that you never use people for your own benefit. It means that you draw out the treasure God has buried deep within them.

> *"If you have a real friend, he is going to have an uplifting, sharpening influence. He is going to make you a better person."*
> **Adrian Rogers**

Day 55

Helping Others Finish Well

The tongue can bring death or life.
Proverbs 18:21a

You need me and I need you. When I am struggling, I need you to encourage me. When you are struggling, you need me to encourage you. In the race of life, what can you do to help others to cross the finish line?

There are thousands of charming stories and little anecdotes that float around social media. I loved this one called "Frog Wisdom":

> A group of frogs were traveling through the woods, and two of them fell into a deep pit. All the other frogs gathered around the pit. When they saw how deep the pit was, they told the two frogs that they were as good as dead. The two frogs ignored the comments and tried to jump up out of the pit with all of their might. The other frogs kept telling them to stop, that they were as good as dead. Finally, one of the frogs took heed to what the other frogs were saying and gave up. He fell down and died. The other frog continued to jump up as hard as he could. Once again, the crowd of frogs yelled at him to stop the pain and just die. He jumped even harder and finally made it out. When he got out, the other frogs said, "Did you not hear us?" The frog explained to them that he

was deaf. He thought they were encouraging him the entire time.

Though the story is a fable, it teaches biblical truths. The power of both life and death is in the tongue. An encouraging word to someone who is down can lift them up and help them make it through the day. A destructive word can be what it takes to kill them. Be careful of what you say. Speak life. Speak hope.

Another story is told of a little girl who desperately wanted a part in her school play. When the parts were announced, she was disappointed to hear that she didn't get one. A wise teacher came beside her and said that she, indeed, had a huge part. She was told she was given the huge role of clapping and cheering while the others were performing.

When you get to heaven, you will find out awards are not given out the same way they are on earth. In the race of life, clapping and cheering are as important as running.

"You need to learn how to speak words of victory, words of praise, words of strength. You can bless with your words or curse with your words. I wonder what kind of a blessing or what kind of a curse you are bringing on your loved ones?"
Adrian Rogers

Day 56

I Have a Hunch He Wants Your Lunch

Then Jesus took the loaves, gave thanks to God, and distributed them to the people. Afterward He did the same with the fish. And they all ate as much as they wanted.
John 6:11

There's an amazing app you can use for recipes these days. You input all the ingredients currently in your pantry, and then the app generates potential recipes using only what you already have. If I were to use that app right now, I would be able to serve a salt and ketchup casserole for dinner! That's my reality, but in my fantasy world, there would never again be a need to go to the grocery store.

Jesus was faced with this same situation. He was teaching a large and hungry crowd with no McDonald's in sight. John 6:5–6 says, "Jesus soon saw a huge crowd of people coming to look for Him. Turning to Philip, He asked, 'Where can we buy bread to feed all these people?' He was testing Philip, for He already knew what He was going to do."

Why would Jesus ask a question when He already knew the answer? Jesus didn't need their advice. And He certainly didn't need their instructions. His only interest was to know if they trusted Him.

With you, He wants to know if you are willing to give Him the meager resources and talents you possess. Philip failed the test. He looked at the calculator and concluded it wasn't possible. On the other hand, when Jesus asked Andrew the same question, Andrew didn't add up what it would take. Instead, Andrew offered what he had, even though he knew it wasn't enough. He said, "There's a young boy here with five barley loaves and two fish. But what good is that with this huge crowd?" (John 6:9).

Jesus didn't want the disciples to perform the miracle. He wanted to know if they were willing to give what they had and watch *Him* perform the miracle. In the early 1980s at a Nationwide Women's Conference at Bellevue Baptist Church I heard Jill Briscoe say something I have never forgotten. With a twinkle in her eye she said, "I have a hunch He wants your lunch."

There is something else I love about this passage almost as much as the feeding of the multitude. I love that the passage says they "ate as much as they wanted" (v. 11). I love it even more when it says there were twelve basketfuls left over. Each disciple got to take home a doggie bag!

When Jesus is involved, there are always leftovers for you to share with others. You don't lose what you give to God; you multiply it.

"There is no problem too big for God to solve.
And there is no person too small for God to use."
Adrian Rogers

Day 57

Is Your Mind Out of Alignment?

*You will keep in perfect peace all who trust in You,
all whose thoughts are fixed on You!*
Isaiah 26:3

When your tires are out of alignment, they pull to the left or the right. You may not know exactly what it is, but you can sense something isn't right. The same thing that happens to your tires happens to your mind. It begins to go in wrong directions. Your default thinking will be the indicator of whether you are out of alignment. Is it automatically going to Christ, or is it going elsewhere? Like your car, it isn't going to get better on its own. More time won't help. More time will only make it worse. You must proactively do something to regain control and get your mind back into alignment with the peace of God. It will be similar to resetting your mind to the original factory settings, or the original way God intended for you to think.

The answer to perfect mental alignment is found in Isaiah 26:3. I love the way the King James Version puts it. It says, "Thou wilt keep him in perfect peace, whose mind is stayed on Thee." In other words, if you think about something over and over other than Jesus, it will take root in your mind, destroy your peace, and warp your perspective.

Why do you listen to the toxicity of other people and allow putrid thoughts to take root and take over like kudzu? Why do the lies and erroneous statements of others bother you so much that they affect your mood, your mind, and your manners? Why do you repeatedly rehearse everything you perceive to be an injustice? Why do you let circumstances beyond your control keep you from pursuing the things you can control? All these things do is allow the weeds to choke out the flowers. They not only steal your personal joy, but they also cloud your spiritual sensitivity to the needs of others.

Weeds in your mind will grow so out of proportion that you will not be able to think straight. Distractions will become obsessions. Don't let Satan use your mind for his playground. If you find this happening, you need an immediate heavenly tune-up. You need a massive dose of God's Word. Reflect on it, memorize it, obey it. Recognize and replace lies.

> *"You can't get this peace from a bottle; you can't get it from a syringe. You can't get it from a psychiatrist, a well-meaning friend, or a book. You can only find your peace in Jesus."*
> **Adrian Rogers**

Day 58

Become a Stronger Leader

Remember your leaders who taught you the word of God. Think of all the good that has come from their lives, and follow the example of their faith.
Hebrews 13:7

How do you become a leader worth following?

Deepen your character. Just as spending time in the sun will darken the pigment of your skin, spending time in the presence of the Son will develop the depth of your character. It will just happen. People will be able to tell. You may not even recognize yourself.

Expand your comfort zone. You are capable of doing more. You are capable of being more. The writer of 1 Chronicles says that a man named Jabez was more honorable than any of his brothers. You can have that said of you. First Chronicles 4:10 says of Jabez: "He was the one who prayed to the God of Israel. 'Oh, that You would bless me and expand my territory! Please be with me in all that I do, and keep me from all trouble and pain!' And God granted him his request." Obviously, God is interested in expanding your territory. The things you are capable of happen inside your comfort zone; the things only God can do happen outside of your comfort zone. Your fear will keep you spiritually stunted. Flip the switch from fear to faith and watch your influence expand.

Increase your knowledge. You become obsolete and out of touch when you stop learning. Not knowing something doesn't mean you can't learn it. Over time, reading one hour a day on any subject will make you an expert in that area. Second Timothy 2:15 says: "Work hard so you can present yourself to God and receive His approval. Be a good worker, one who does not need to be ashamed and who correctly explains the word of truth."

A daily devotional time with God is a starting place, but a mighty spiritual leader needs to go even deeper. Seek out the mentorship of mature leaders in the faith. When you do, listen more than you talk. Make time to read great Christian nonfiction books. It will get your spiritual juices flowing. It will put new thoughts in your mind that will stretch you. There is no doubt that leaders are readers. In addition, there is a treasure trove of wealth on podcasts and recorded sermons. I can continue to glean the wisdom of my father, Adrian Rogers, anytime at LWF.org even though he is in heaven. Don't just listen; take notes. Apply what you learn. Learn from godly men and women who are committed to the inerrancy of Scripture and the preeminence of Christ. If you do these things, your leadership ability will increase. Your influence will grow. Your ministry will multiply. Your Master will be pleased.

> *"The weakest ink is better than the best memory. Study with pen in hand."*
> **Adrian Rogers**

Day 59

Open Doors and Closed Doors

In everything we do, we show that we are true ministers of God. We patiently endure troubles and hardships and calamities of every kind.
2 Corinthians 6:4

There are a lot of misguided advice-givers who will tell you that the way to determine God's will is to simply walk through any open doors around you—assuming God has leveled the path right to that doorway—and avoid any closed doors. I hope you can see the dangers of that theology. All open doors are not God's will. There are really scary things behind some unlocked doors. All closed doors are not clear indicators that something is not God's will. Some are, but not all. There are far too many times when people mistakenly take the path of least resistance in the name of following God's will.

To be honest, something in my flesh wants the theology of following open doors. It is comforting to think that God is clearing away all my obstacles and unlocking all my doors. Of course, I want God to give me the money I need, friends that will support me, and opportunities that are plopped right down in the middle of my lap. I want to "rest" in the Lord, and I prefer to do it with a glass of lemonade in my hand as I'm sitting in my lounge chair by my swimming pool. I want the Christ life to be like that. That is my fantasy of what is meant by the "abundant life."

We all think life is good when times are good. But little growth takes place when life is easy. The best growth takes place with a covering of fertilizer, often in the form of manure. Are you smelling what I'm stepping in? If God does give smooth pathways, it is only because He knows we are going to need rest for the tedious journey that lies ahead. He knows we will need our strength for the battle that will be fought tomorrow.

When the going gets hard, can you thank God that the construction zone you find yourself in the middle of is God working on you? He is making you more like Him, rather than clearing a path for you to live a life of ease that doesn't need Him.

> *"It is a very shallow theology that says if we're in the will of God, that we're just going to sail smoothly on the sea of life. We'll have no sickness, no sorrow, no disappointment, no separation. There'll be no death in our family. There'll be no problems. This is the gospel of cash and Cadillacs. Friend, there's a Greek word for that and it's baloney."*
> **Adrian Rogers**

Day 60

Humility Is the Key

You must have the same attitude that Christ Jesus had.
Philippians 2:5

Humility leads the list of essential attitudes you must have to be like Jesus. Philippians 2:6–7a says, "Though He was God, He did not think of equality with God as something to cling to. Instead, He gave up His divine privileges." Jesus Christ is Almighty God. He is glorious, limitless, and unfathomably powerful, yet He voluntarily set it all aside to enter earth as a helpless baby, born in a smelly stable. If you have accomplishments and titles on earth, it only means you have a higher stewardship to use your influence to impact others. Use it as a platform to serve rather than a pedestal you stand on to be admired.

You can't be like Jesus without a servant attitude. Philippians 2:7b–8 says, "He took the humble position of a slave and was born as a human being. When He appeared in human form, He humbled himself in obedience to God and died a criminal's death on a cross." The Creator of the universe not only humbled himself by taking the body of a man, but he chose, as a man, not to be a powerful or prominent man. He chose to be a servant. And not simply a servant but a servant who would die an unspeakably cruel and painful death, a servant who would die this death for sins He did not commit, so that you could receive the forgiveness you do not deserve.

If you want to be like Jesus, you must have what one of my mentors, Randy Draper, calls a "happy to do it" attitude. It's the motto of Randy's life, and it's why I hang on his every word. Philippians 2:14 says, "Do everything without complaining and arguing." Did you know that there is far more to servanthood than doing the right things? It is doing the right things with a "happy to do it" attitude. Now that's where it gets hard. A true servant is someone who wants to serve, instead of having to serve. A true servant looks for ways to inconvenience herself. A true servant serves even when a thoughtless, selfish person expects to be served. Servanthood is not doing something so you can pose for a photo op.

It's okay to have an "attitude" if you have the attitude of Christ!

"Do you want to be like Jesus?
Jesus came as a servant."
Adrian Rogers

Day 61

It's Already in Your Closet

*By His divine power, God has given us
everything we need for living a godly life.*
2 Peter 1:3a

I saw some shoes I really wanted. They looked warm and comfy, and my feet were cold and sore. I couldn't find anywhere to purchase them. I eventually found a pair in the wrong size, and I wanted these particular shoes so much that I almost bought them anyway and thought I would just pull my toes in a bit. Ha! I was so frustrated that I purchased two pairs that were kind of similar but not the same. Even after I bought those two pairs, I continued to search. It dawned on me that I could look on eBay. On eBay, I bought three more pairs of gross, used shoes. What is wrong with me? Why did I do that? Note to self or anyone else reading: don't buy used shoes on eBay!

What is the point? The point is that after I spent hours and hours looking for the exact shoes I wanted, and then purchased five pairs of shoes that weren't what I was looking for, one day I was looking in my closet, and there they were! That's right. I found the exact pair I had been searching for. They were in perfect condition! They were sitting in my *own* closet. They were already in my possession!

You know what I'm going to say next. What about you? First Peter 1:3–4 says, "By His divine power, God has given us everything we need for living a godly life. We have received all of this by coming to know Him, the One who called us to Himself by means of His marvelous glory and excellence. And because of His glory and excellence, He has given us great and precious promises. These are the promises that enable you to share his divine nature and escape the world's corruption caused by human desires." Ephesians 1:3 says, "All praise to God, the Father of our Lord Jesus Christ, who has blessed us with every spiritual blessing in the heavenly realms because we are united with Christ."

Do you see it? There is nothing you could possibly want that you don't already have. Every spiritual blessing is already yours. Quit looking for the things of this world that are cheap counterfeits and will never satisfy. Go to your prayer closet. That's where you will find what you already possess.

> *"Everything—oh, please listen—everything that you need to live the Christian life, you already have if you have Jesus. You say, 'Well, then why don't I have it?' It is because you have not possessed your possessions. The devil doesn't want you to learn what you have in the Lord Jesus."*
> **Adrian Rogers**

Day 62

Character Qualities That Will Increase Your Influence

And you should imitate me, just as I imitate Christ.
1 Corinthians 11:1

What are some of the qualities that will help people to see Jesus in you more clearly?

Persuasion. People are drawn by your life, but your life is never enough. You have to use words. Your life leaves a good impression. Your words will enable them to make decisions. The words you use have to be words that attract. If it is an important conversation, you need to think it through and pray it out. Important words should be carefully crafted, not casually spouted.

Patience. Wait for God's timing. Stick with the process and the person for as long as it takes. Do not get irritated by the failures, slowness, and inconvenience created by those you seek to influence. How long does it take for God to get through to you?

Gentleness. If you are trying to get people to change, you must realize they have reasons for not wanting to. You must handle the fears, insecurities, and vulnerabilities that people may confide in you with utmost care and tenderness. If you don't, they will never confide in you again. Most of the time you only get one chance. Be thoughtful in the little things. They will be remembered even more than big things.

Knowledge. Know what you are talking about before you open your mouth. People who "know" things that aren't true don't have a lot of respect. Study the subject. Take the time. And the more knowledge you obtain, the more humble you need to become. Being smart and arrogant is even worse than not knowing. In addition, you should value the insight of the people you are trying to influence as much or more than you value imposing your opinion on them. Never jump to conclusions or form opinions without gathering the facts. And always give the benefit of the doubt.

Unconditional Love. Always love people. Never pressure them. Listen without condemning, criticizing, or ridiculing. This is the only atmosphere in which growth and change will occur. Your goal is to influence, not to win an argument.

Pure Motives. You should have no desire, spoken or unspoken, to deceive, take advantage of, manipulate, or control. There should be no secret agendas. Your only goal should be the good of everyone and the glory of God.

"I would be a sheer, unmitigated fool to stand up here and try to preach with a heart that is not clean and not pure."
Adrian Rogers

Day 63

If You Are Sold, You Will Be Bold

"We cannot stop telling about everything we have seen and heard."
Acts 4:20

If your faith isn't real, don't try to export it. Sir Winston Churchill eloquently said, "Before you can inspire with emotion, you must be swamped with it yourself. Before you can move their tears, your own must flow. To convince them, you must yourself, believe."[9] People are starved for answers, and they will desperately seek out anyone who has found them. If you have no passion for your own faith, don't try to pawn it off on somebody else. All you will do is turn them off. You will be labeled a hypocrite.

John Maxwell said, "Your passion and conviction must be more compelling than your words. The first person who should be excited about your vision is you."[10] To be convincing, you must be convinced. If Jesus hasn't changed your life, you better make sure you know Him. It is impossible to be a Christian without having a changed life. Second Corinthians 5:16b–17, "At one time we thought of Christ merely from a human point of view. How differently we know Him now! This means that anyone who belongs to Christ has become a new person. The old life is gone; a new life has begun!"

Acts 4:13 says, "The members of the council were amazed when they saw the boldness of Peter and John, for they could see that they were ordinary men with no special training in the Scriptures. They also recognized them as men who had been with Jesus." Peter and John weren't bold because their education and training made them confident. They were bold because their lives had been changed. A man with a testimony is an unstoppable force. Acts 4:18–20 says, "So they called the apostles back in and commanded them never again to speak or teach in the name of Jesus. But Peter and John replied, 'Do you think God wants us to obey you rather than Him? We cannot stop telling about everything we have seen and heard.'"

If you are sold, you will be bold.

> *"I am convinced there is not a whole lot wrong in America that could not be radically, dramatically, and swiftly put back in place if all across America we had a generation of preachers who would open the Word of God, filled with the Spirit of God, and preach the Christ of God, without fear or intimidation or worry about being politically correct."*
> **Adrian Rogers**

Day 64

Is Your Elevator Going Up or Down?

"The LORD doesn't see things the way you see them. People judge by outward appearance, but the LORD looks at the heart."
1 Samuel 16:7b

On a scale of one to ten, what level of spiritual maturity do you think pleases God the most? The answer to that question is, "It depends." If level 1 is going up and level 10 is going down, then the person at level 1 is the one with whom God is pleased. It's not where you are, it's where you are headed.

How long does it take to get right with God? I didn't say, How long does it take to be spiritually mature? I said, How long does it take to get right with God? It doesn't happen over the years. It happens instantly. In a mere second, at any stage of sinfulness and degradation, you can repent and turn from your sin. In a blink, you can be in perfect fellowship and right standing with your Savior.

What is repentance? It doesn't involve years of Bible study, church attendance, and penance. It is coming face-to-face with the horrific nature of your sin. What is needed first is confession and then turning and going in the opposite direction. It doesn't matter where you are when you turn; what matters is that you turn. A prostitute who repents and turns is as clean as a preacher standing in the pulpit.

This makes it really hard to judge. Someone who is all cleaned up on the outside might be the person who has just hardened their heart and pressed the down button. Someone else who may have lived a life of debauchery could have just turned from their sin to follow the Savior and pressed the up button. It's what goes on inside that changes a person's direction. First Samuel 16 says, "The Lord doesn't see things the way you see them. People judge by outward appearance, but the Lord looks at the heart" (v. 7b).

Remember, though, that someone may be saved from the gutter, but they will not stay that way. Eventually, people will see on the outside what happened in an instance on the inside.

Are you weighed down with guilt and hopelessness? Fifteen seconds from now you can be clean.

"It is not enough to confess sin without forsaking it."
Adrian Rogers

Day 65

When Submission Is Difficult to Understand

For the Lord's sake, respect all human authority.
1 Peter 2:13a

Submission to authority is not always easy to do. There are many times when it is difficult to understand. You might find yourself in one of three hard situations the book of First Peter mentions:

A Godless Government. I know that you won't always agree with the person who gets elected. You may not have noted for them. In Peter's time the emperor was Nero. History says he was one of the most ruthless, perverted men who ever lived. And yet, Peter says in 1 Peter 2:13–14a, "For the Lord's sake, respect all human authority–whether the king as head of state, or the officials he has appointed." Remember that when asked to do something immoral you must always obey God. But the truth is that generally you are simply asked to do things you don't want to do, rather than things God has outright forbidden. Do those things, for the Lord's sake.

An Unreasonable or Unjust Master (or Boss). Peter goes on to say in 1 Peter 2:18–19, "You who are slaves must accept the authority of your masters with all respect. Do what they tell you—not only if they are kind and reasonable, but even if they are cruel. For God is pleased when, conscious of his will, you patiently endure unfair treatment." Switch the word employee for slave and apply this verse to your boss. Obey when the boss is looking and when he isn't. Do your work as unto the Lord.

An Unsaved or Disobedient Husband. First Peter 3:1–2 says, "In the same way, you wives must accept the authority of your husbands. Then, even if some refuse to obey the Good News, your godly lives will speak to them without any words. They will be won over by observing your pure and reverent lives." In cases of abuse, you need to get to a place of safety. But if you simply don't like or respect the man you are living with, Peter doesn't give any wiggle room.

Jesus, our example, did not retaliate when He was insulted or threaten revenge when He suffered. He left His case in the hands of God, who always judges fairly (1 Pet. 2:23). This is pretty clear-cut. I don't like it any more than you do. It's hard. But I do trust God. He will give grace.

"It was the submissive spirit of the early Christians that turned the Roman Empire upside down."
Adrian Rogers

Day 66

He Knows Your Name

The Lord replied to Moses, "I will indeed do what you have asked, for I look favorably on you, and I know you by name."
Exodus 33:17

The God who created the universe knows you by name! Both of those facts are equally astonishing. You are not a nameless number. You are an intimate friend. Psalm 139:1–6 says,

> O Lord, You have examined my heart and know everything about me. You know when I sit down or stand up. You know my thoughts even when I'm far away. You see me when I travel and when I rest at home. You know everything I do. You know what I am going to say even before I say it, Lord. You go before me and follow me. You place Your hand of blessing on my head. Such knowledge is too wonderful for me, too great for me to understand.

Read it again. Read it out loud. The Lord knows every little, intimate detail about you. He knows every freckle, every mole, and for some of you, every tattoo. He knows every secret, shameful thing you have ever done or thought. And He loves you still. He also knows every secret, selfless thing you have done that no one else has even noticed. And He will reward you for it. He knows what you are going to do before you do it. He knows where you have been hurt and wounded. He knows what will bless you and bring you joy. He knows you and He knows you by name. He doesn't just love mankind; He loves you. You! He loves you!

Jesus knows every secret and loves you still. He doesn't draw back in disgust. He didn't choose you, and then you did something that made Him regret His choice. He knew what you would do before He chose you. I can promise that Satan doesn't want you to know that.

He also knows every wonderful thing about you. He knows all the goodness that is in your heart. He knows everything you wish you could do for others. He knows the tenderness in your spirit. He can hear the holy thoughts that stir your soul. He tailor-made you for a special purpose and assignment you can do better than anyone else on earth.

I pray you can feel it. If you ever feel unloved or unlovable, you can rest assured that it didn't come from God. You can rebuke it. You can know for sure that God loves you exactly as you are. But you can also know for sure that He loves you too much to allow you to stay there. He is on your side and will help you become whom you need to be. He will do it because you are His intimate friend.

"You are on Jesus's prayer list. The Lord Jesus knows you by name, and He calls you by name."
Adrian Rogers

Day 67

What Happens When You Submit to Someone Who Is Undeserving?

So anyone who rebels against authority is rebelling against what God has instituted, and they will be punished.
Romans 13:2

Previously I shared that as a Christian you are called to submit, not just to those who are godly but also to those who are unreasonable and unkind. What will result from this kind of voluntary, joyful, and uncompromising submission?

God will be glorified. First Peter 2:13a: "For the Lord's sake, respect all human authority." First Peter 2:19: "For God is pleased when, conscious of his will, you patiently endure unfair treatment." From these and other Scriptures, there is no doubt that submission is God's desire, and it pleases Him. You need no other reason.

You will be like Christ. First Peter 2:21: "For God called you to do good, even if it means suffering, just as Christ suffered for you. He is your example, and you must follow in His steps." Remember WWJD? "What would Jesus do?" It's right out of Scripture, big and plain.

The lost will be won. First Peter 2:12: "Be careful to live properly among your unbelieving neighbors. Then even if they accuse you of doing wrong, they will see your honorable behavior, and they will give honor to God when He judges the world." First Peter 3:1–2: "In the same way, you wives must accept the authority of your husbands. Then, even if some refuse to obey the Good News, your godly lives will speak to them without any words. They will be won over by observing your pure and reverent lives." How can rebelling against any inconvenient command be more important to you than the salvation of a soul? The lost world is watching.

You will be fulfilled. First Peter 3:4: "You should clothe yourselves instead with the beauty that comes from within, the unfading beauty of a gentle and quiet spirit, which is so precious to God." Isn't it amazing that submission is the only way to fulfillment and peace? I know that for me, personally, when I rebel, my stomach is in knots all day. It is in knots even though I got my way. But when I obey, the very thing I didn't want to do amazingly becomes a source of joy. God's ways are like that. If you don't believe me, try it.

"Submission is one equal voluntarily placing himself under another equal that God may thereby be glorified."
Adrian Rogers

Day 68

Do What You Said You Would Do

Keep their promises even when it hurts.
Psalm 15:4b

Integrity is doing what you said you would do, long after the mood you said you would do it in has left you. I am sad to say that we live in a culture where people change their minds if a better offer comes along. They think nothing of it. If you, as a Christian, have signed a contract, shaken a hand, or made a promise, then that promise needs to be kept, regardless of what box seats to any championship game or big-ticket concert was offered to you after your promise was made. You need to keep your commitment regardless of how much more someone else says they are willing to pay. You need to keep your obligation regardless of how much more fun the new group of people is going to be. It's a biblical principle. Your character is at stake.

Reliability and trustworthiness are two of the greatest marks of Christ-centered leadership. If you say you will do something, people need to *know* you are going to do it. It doesn't depend on your mood, the inconvenience of what you promised, or whether you get a better offer.

Obviously, some emergencies arise where commitments need to be changed. But I believe your integrity is at stake when you change your promises out of preference. Regardless of whether it is a change because of an emergency or because of preference, either way, you need to make certain you offer an equal, or preferably a better, substitute than the original promise.

Integrity applies to all areas of life. The New Testament principle taught by Jesus Himself in the Sermon on the Mount is found in Matthew 5:33–37a, "You have also heard that our ancestors were told, 'You must not break your vows; you must carry out the vows you make to the Lord. . . . But I tell you, don't take an oath at all! . . . rather, simply 'let your yes mean yes, and your no mean no.'" In short, your word alone should be strong enough that having to swear you'll make good on it isn't necessary. A broken promise whether it is in the form of a contract or simply an ordinary commitment is a lie. It isn't simply something that happens in the common course of life that is no big deal.

A good rule of thumb on anything is to keep your word, and when you make a promise, always underpromise and overdeliver. That's a good word for a successful business and an even better word for a successful life.

"What you do should agree with what you say."
Adrian Rogers

Day 69

Making a Connection

*Many will see what He has done and be amazed.
They will put their trust in the LORD.*
Psalm 40:3

When God does a work in your spirit and God's activity in your life is current and fresh, there will be a spiritual connection that can be compared to an electrical current flowing between people. It may not be able to be seen, but it definitely can be felt. The spirit of the person with whom you are sharing can feel the genuineness of your relationship with God. The Holy Spirit's work in your life overflows from your life and ignites a spark of faith in another life. If what you are sharing isn't authentic, the same effect is not there.

When you keep current, there will be a current. There will be a connection. When people can sense the working of God in your life, they will ask questions. Your faith will create an attraction in people who are searching for answers. As people begin to open up, the Holy Spirit will supernaturally give you the answers they are seeking.

You can't prepare in advance for all the questions someone might ask. That is so sterile. Your job is to share what God has done for you. If it is genuine, you don't have to rehearse. Your job is to give Him glory, to give Him credit, and to give Him praise.

If you find that someone is even mildly interested in what you are sharing, find out what caused that bit of curiosity. When you find that out, you will have located the place in their life where God is at work.

Ask God to take the conversation over and allow the Holy Spirit to speak through you. All you need to do is show them how He can do for them what He has done for you. You can't study for this. You have to have a real, active, current relationship with Jesus for it to take place.

What do you need to do to get these types of conversations started? Just make it a habit to verbally give God glory for what He has done and then actively listen to how others respond. If you don't share and don't listen, it is no wonder nothing happens. But when you do share and do listen for responses, you will be able to meet people where they are and offer hope exactly where they hurt. A spiritual connection between spirits will take place.

People all around you are looking for answers. You create an atmosphere that is conducive to sharing when you are vulnerable about what God is doing in you.

> *"Evangelism is just one beggar telling another beggar where to find bread."*
> **Adrian Rogers, quoting Martin Luther**

Day 70

Be a Praise Detective

We always thank God for all of you and pray for you constantly. As we pray to our God and Father about you, we think of your faithful work, your loving deeds, and the enduring hope you have because of our Lord Jesus Christ.
1 Thessalonians 1:2–3

People come in two types. They are either encouragers or depleters. It's easy to tell the difference. One type puts energy into you. The other takes energy out of you. One person looks for what you are doing right. The other person looks for what you are doing wrong. One says, "I've got you. You can count on me to lift you up." The other says, "Gotcha! You can count on me to call you out."

In Kenneth Blanchard's great business book *The One Minute Manager,* he says you can increase the productivity and improve the attitude of your employees with just one minute of your time every day. I like anything that only takes one minute, so that got my attention. The secret he shares is: "You should catch someone in the act of doing something right and tell them about it."[11]

This is the opposite of constantly picking at someone by noticing every fault and every shortcoming. How about you? Are you a monitor? Are you the food police? Are you a picker? Do you feel that it is your calling to point out to your husband, roommate, or friend how they can do something better? Do you feel like you are being a good mother when you focus on all the things your children are doing wrong? Do you feel like your "spiritual gift" is discernment and you define that gift as a calling from God to notice faults? You do need to be a detective. But you need to be a detective who is diligently searching out things to praise.

You see what you are looking for. In a relationship, most people are basically 80 percent pleasant. They really are trying. However, if you focus on the 20 percent of a person that is unpleasant, then in your mind, that 20 percent becomes exaggerated and becomes 80 percent to you. Focus always blows something out of proportion.

Change your focus. See people as Christ sees them. See who they are in Him. See who they can be because of Jesus. Look at them through His eyes.

"You will never know the ripple that will touch the shore of eternity when you drop the stone of grace into somebody's heart."
Adrian Rogers

Day 71

One Size Fits All

Let all that I am praise the LORD;
with my whole heart, I will praise His holy name.
Psalm 103:1

I enjoy unique people. People watching is like going to the zoo. If you go to the zoo, I'm not sure which is more interesting, the animals inside the cages or the people outside the cages. I think quirky, odd people are fascinating. My spirit fights against cookie-cutter people. People who think all Christians should be the same cause an inner conflict in me. Give me delightfully different any day. I had a friend who called them "God's colorful people."

My husband, Mike, loves to tell the story of asking my father if he could marry me. He claims my father's response was: "Mike, do you realize Gayle is different?" Well, I can promise you that if he didn't realize it then, he realizes it now! I am different. I look at things from a different perspective than most people. I see things that others don't see. One of my friends told me that my brain synapses were different from anyone else on the earth. Unfortunately, I sometimes say things that no one else says. I told Mike, "Everyone was thinking it." He replied, "That may be true, but you were the only one saying it." I find humor in everything. Many times I am the only one laughing. Many times no one else even gets what I said. What's wrong with them?

That brings me to the questions: Does complete surrender mean that you give up your personality? When you die to yourself, do you die to your perspective, your creativity, your humor, the idiosyncrasies that make you, you? The answer is completely, absolutely, positively NO!

Let me put it this way. One of the many things I find humor in are pieces of clothing that are labeled "One Size Fits All." I could go on and on about that. But, even if, even if you could get that pair of pants on everyone's body, there is no way they look like the same pants. There is one thing for sure that pants are not, and that is "One Size Fits All." But Jesus is! Jesus can put absolutely anyone on and wear them like a glove. But when He puts you on, like those pants, He looks different on you than He looks on anyone else. You retain every bit of your uniqueness. He likes the way He created you. He made you that way for a special purpose.

I want to praise God with *all* that I am. I want to praise Him with all that I am, in all my uniqueness. Every part of me. I want to glorify Him by allowing Him to inhabit me in such a way that the world can see a version of Jesus lived out through me that they can't see anywhere else. That would make you and me pretty important, wouldn't it?

> *"God made us different that*
> *He might make us one."*
> **Adrian Rogers**

Day 72

Quit Serving God Leftovers

*Honor the L*ORD *with your wealth and with the best part of everything you produce. Then He will fill your barns with grain, and your vats will overflow with good wine.*
Proverbs 3:9–10

Are you giving God your best? Are you honoring Him first? Order matters! Matthew 6:33: "But seek first the kingdom of God and His righteousness, and all these things shall be added to you" (NKJV).

There are so many convicting applications of seeking God first and giving Him the best part. Think about your finances. You may indeed tithe. The question is: When do you do it? Do you take care of your bills first? That's serving God leftovers. That's ignoring the principle of "firstfruits." God doesn't need your money. God wants your heart. He wants your trust. Giving to Him first proves that you trust that He will provide for the rest of your needs. Giving to Him first shows that you believe He is able. Giving to Him last proves that you were able. That's all the difference in the world.

What about your time? Have you heard someone say, "When I get home at night, I'm too mentally and physically exhausted to do anything else." If you don't meet with God in the first part of your day, don't you realize that puts Him into the part of your day where you have nothing left? How can you seek God's direction for your day if you are talking with Him after it has already happened? You are attempting to run your spiritual engine on fumes. If you don't dress yourself in the armor of God before you go into battle, you are wide open for the attack of the Enemy all day long. Order matters.

What about your mind? Do you check your social media feed, texts, emails, stock market updates, and news releases first? Be honest with yourself. Do you? Refusing to check these other things first is difficult. When your phone "dings," it is hard not to look. Let me ask this: If there isn't time for anything else, what is the one thing you do in the morning? Is your coffee more important than Christ to begin your day? Which would affect you most if you missed? If you will "seek first the kingdom of God," then God will take care of everything else. If you will go before Him first, then He will go before you.

> *"Give God what's right, not what's left."*
> **Adrian Rogers**

Day 73

The Hopelessness of Shame

Suddenly, a man with leprosy approached Him and knelt before Him. "Lord," the man said, "If You are willing, You can heal me and make me clean." Jesus reached out and touched him. "I am willing," He said. "Be healed!" And instantly the leprosy disappeared.
Matthew 8:2–3

Two of the saddest words in the English language are *hopelessness* and *shame*. Shame drives you into a dark pit of isolation and despair. Satan's choicest tool is to whisper your vilest thoughts into your ear over and over again, until you are crushed under their humiliating weight and feel as if there is no escape. Even if there were an escape, he makes you feel that you wouldn't deserve it.

In the Bible, leprosy is symbolic of shame. Lepers were isolated outside of the camp. If they were to ever come into a public arena, they were required to shout, "Unclean! Unclean!" everywhere they went to warn people to stay away. They had no hope, no cure, and no longer any human touch.

The story told in Matthew 8:2–3 is one of the most stunning stories in the New Testament. The last thing the crowd expected was a vile, disgusting leper in their midst. But "suddenly," before anyone could stop him, a leper approached Jesus, and with one of the greatest displays of faith in the Bible, this leper said to Him, "Lord, if you are willing, You can heal me and make me clean." Jesus didn't recoil in repulsion. He gently said, "I am willing." And then He did the unthinkable. He "touched him." Immediately he was healed. This is the first time in the Bible that anyone ever touched a leper!

Have you done something that has filled you with such shame that you feel unforgivable? I am reminded of the words to "He Touched Me," by Bill and Gloria Gaither: "Shackled by a heavy burden, 'Neath a load of guilt and shame. Then the hand of Jesus touched me. And now I am no longer the same."[12]

Dear friend, nothing you have ever done makes Jesus unwilling to touch you. Your shame can be erased in an instant. Just ask. He is willing! Ephesians 2:12b–13 says, "You lived in this world without God and without hope. But now you have been united with Christ Jesus. Once you were far away from God, but now you have been brought near to Him through the blood of Christ." Hallelujah! That is a beautiful verse!

"For a multitude of sins, there is a multitude of mercies."
Adrian Rogers

Day 74

My Mother Could Eat All the Jelly She Wanted

So we praise God for the glorious grace He has poured out on us who belong to His dear Son.
Ephesians 1:6

My grandfather, Guston Gentry, was a quiet man. Because he was so reserved, I didn't know him that well. My mother has so wanted me to appreciate him that she has told me on several different occasions how generous he was. To illustrate that, she said that when she was growing up, he would always let her have all the jelly she wanted. I have always thought that was hilarious. Now, realize, it doesn't take much to make me laugh. But suffice it to say, I've never said, "Pass the jelly," without that coming into my mind.

If more jelly is one of your primary needs in life, then that is a great thing. But more jelly isn't my primary need. Actually, I suspect that more jelly has been more my problem than my need. I don't want to downplay the generosity of my grandfather. I am certain that in the Great Depression that was, indeed, a big deal.

In contrast, I was reading about the generosity of my heavenly Father. There are two things He gives generously. They are grace and forgiveness. Ephesians 1:6 in the NIV puts it this way: "To the praise of his glorious grace, which he has freely given us in the One he loves." This grace that is available to you has two aspects to it; each one is equally wonderful.

There is saving grace where God redeems you, even though you are completely undeserving. It doesn't matter what you have done. There is enough grace to cover all your sins. But there is also living grace, where God gives you the ability and the desire to do what you ought to do. Both aspects of this grace are given freely, without reserve. It is constantly available.

And think about this. He always gives more than is needed, so that it can overflow into the lives of others. You don't have to hold back because you may need to keep some grace in reserve. If God only gave you enough grace for yourself, there wouldn't be enough left over to give grace to others when they offend. You don't have to worry. There is plenty of it. So go to your generous Father and get a big, ole heapin' helping!

"If it will make you healthy, happy, holy, or wholesome, God says, 'Help yourself!'"
Adrian Rogers

Day 75

Do the Work

"Be strong and courageous, and do the work. Don't be afraid or discouraged, for the LORD God, my God, is with you. He will not fail you or forsake you."
1 Chronicles 28:20

First Chronicles is such a great book! If you aren't careful, you might miss it, because chapters 1–9 are nothing but lists of impossible-to-pronounce names. But even that part is encouraging. God is interested in your name and what you do whether you are Joab, who was in charge of the king's army, or Jehdeiah, who was in charge of the king's donkeys.

This year I read the book of 1 Chronicles differently. I didn't skim or fast-forward. I tried (emphasis on "tried") to pronounce each name out loud as I slowly made my way through. I told myself that there was not a single insignificant person. God carefully called each one of them by their name. Hazarmaveth's name, my name, and your name are all important to Him.

The families they came from were also important. They didn't choose their families. God did. God chose Adrian Rogers to be my father. I know you probably wish he had been yours. But believe me, there were many times when I wished He hadn't chosen him to be mine. That's a hard one to live up to. In 1 Chronicles 23:6, it says that David divided the Levites into divisions named after the descendants of the three sons of Levi: the Gershonites, the Kohathites, and the Merarites. Each division had different tasks. I know you don't have to have the profession your parents do, thank goodness, but I still wrote in the margin of my Bible, "I'm an Adrianite." It's important to represent him well. Feel sorry for me!

In 1 Chronicles 28:20, Solomon was assigned the responsibility of building the temple by his father, King David. That's even heavier than being Adrian Rogers's child! Can you imagine his fear and feeling of inadequacy? But his father, King David, said, "Be strong and courageous and do the work. Don't be afraid or discouraged, for the Lord God, my God is with you. He will not fail you or forsake you." You may have a great family legacy to live up to, or you may need to be the one to begin one. Lean on God! Fulfill your calling! Do the work! He will not fail you or forsake you.

"God's plan is to take ordinary people with ordinary talents, do extraordinary things through them, and give glory to Himself."
Adrian Rogers

Day 76

Finding Happiness

*Make me walk along the path of Your commands,
for that is where my happiness is found.*
Psalm 119:35

For years, I have had a restless spirit created by an unceasing search for happiness. The tragedy is that all of the things I thought would make me happy are the things that brought me bondage. The areas I put before God are the areas where I unwittingly gave Satan an idolatrous foothold in my life, which he used to enslave and control me.

I have gone through several stages in my life. The first stage was a stage of grasping and clinging to the things I thought would meet my needs. I wrongly thought I had to have these things to make me happy. I grasped them tightly and desperately. Of course, I did. I didn't think I could live without them.

The second stage was wanting to serve God but hoping I could do so without having to give these things up. I dreaded that I would be required to relinquish control of certain areas that were not beneficial for my growth or God's glory. I thought that giving them up would make me miserable. In this second stage, I was torn between two worlds, attempting to serve two masters.

The third stage was a stage of dying to myself. I finally was overcome with my sinfulness and the idolatry that was in my heart. In this stage, I didn't open up my hands and hope God would not take these idolatrous things out. Instead, I opened my hands and *begged* Him to take them out. I did not want a trace of anything that didn't bring Him glory. With tears of repentance, I asked God to release me of the chains and strongholds of Satan. The things I grasped thinking I had to have to make me happy were actually the things that were causing me misery, defeat, and bondage. I repented of the areas in my life that I had put before God. I bound Satan in those areas and cast him out in the authority of the name of Jesus and His shed blood. Praise God. My chains are gone! I've been set free!

My strongholds are not yours. You know what yours are. You know what you are not willing to release. Satan has been lying to you. They won't make you happy. They will kill you. Psalm 139:24 says, "Point out anything in me that offends You, and lead me along the path of everlasting life."

> *"Every time God says, 'Thou shalt not,'*
> *He's simply saying, 'Don't hurt yourself.'*
> *And every time He says, 'Thou shalt,' He's*
> *saying, 'Help yourself to happiness.'"*
> **Adrian Rogers**

Day 77

Break a Leg

"Come, let us return to the LORD. He has torn us to pieces; now He will heal us. He has injured us; now He will bandage our wounds."
Hosea 6:1

When a sheep was prone to stray from the protection of a shepherd, the shepherd would go after that sheep and intentionally break its legs. He did this not to harm the sheep but to protect it from inevitable death at the hands of a predator. The shepherd would then carry and bind that wounded sheep next to his heart until it was fully and completely healed. The wandering sheep, whose legs had been intentionally broken, was the sheep who ended up with the most intimate relationship with the shepherd. He was the one who was carried next to the shepherd's heart until his healing was complete. Psalm 119:67 says, "I used to wander off until You disciplined me; but now I closely follow Your word." Like that sheep, a loving God may have to break you in order to use you. Rest assured that when you heal, you will be better than before.

Proverbs 27:6 says, "Wounds from a sincere friend are better than many kisses from an enemy." Aren't you glad Jesus loves you enough to discipline you and lovingly bring you home? Again, in Hebrews 12:5b–6, 10b–11,

> He said, "My child, don't make light of the LORD's discipline, and don't give up when He corrects you. For the LORD disciplines those He loves, and He punishes

each one He accepts as His child.'... God's discipline is always good for us, so that we might share in His holiness. No discipline is enjoyable while it is happening—it is painful! But afterward there will be a peaceful harvest of right living for those who are trained in this way."

This is beautifully expressed by Robert Robinson who wrote the words to the beautiful hymn, "Come Thou Fount," and John Wyeth who put them to music:

> Jesus sought me when a stranger, Wand'ring from the fold of God,
> He, to rescue me from danger, interposed His precious blood,
> O to grace how great a debtor Daily I'm constrained to be!
> Let Thy goodness, like a fetter, Bind my wandering heart to Thee.
> Prone to wander, Lord I feel it, Prone to leave the God I love.
> Here's my heart, O take and seal it; Seal it for Thy courts above.[13]

> *"The wounded in life are those who have learned difficult lessons. Often their sight is clearer and their perception of God sharper because of the pain they have felt and the healing they have received."*
> **Adrian Rogers**

Day 78

Entrepreneurs for Jesus

*Paul lived and worked with them,
for they were tentmakers just as he was.*
Acts 18:3

Every person who bears the name of Christ is called into the full-time Christian ministry. That means you! It doesn't matter if you are a gospel preacher or a preschool teacher. You are to be a full-time Christian, in full-time ministry. Regardless of your job title, your primary desire should be to be a light in a dark world and to live out godly principles on enemy turf. An entrepreneur for Jesus views each interaction throughout the day with a customer, supplier, employee, or fellow worker as a divine appointment to share the good news of Christ either by word or example. In addition, an entrepreneur for Jesus makes a commitment to use the excess profit they generate as an opportunity to fund kingdom causes and meet the needs of hurting people. Kingdom giving, not lavish living, should be your motivation to generate wealth.

Don't misunderstand. The church certainly needs full-time ministers. May God raise up godly men and women to minister within the church who will feed and equip the members He has equally called to minister outside of the church who are serving on the front lines. The church world, the business world, the service world, and the teaching world all need full-time ministers. May God raise up entrepreneurs for Jesus who are called to be lights "in the midst of a crooked and perverse generation" (Phil. 2:15 NASB).

Let me assure you that God wants to use you right where you are. He wants you to bloom where you are planted. He is calling you to be a light to the person in the cubicle next to you. And if you happen to be in a business that generates a lot of income and God has gifted you with the ability to make that money, He has a task for your life that is beyond your personal comfort and enrichment. You are accountable, as a steward, to be a pipeline God uses to further His kingdom work.

"Your work is to be the temple of your devotion and the platform for your witness."
Adrian Rogers

Day 79

I Am Learning to Love the Wind

"Even the wind and waves obey Him!"
Mark 4:41

When the wind comes, your reaction will depend on whose side you are on. To the ungodly, the wind should rightly be feared as a devastating and destructive power. But to those who know and love the Father, He sends His gentle touch, His loving provision, and His wise direction through the wind. You can feel His presence through the soft and gentle breeze. It is the refreshing touch of the unseen God on our skin. Sit outside. Breathe it in. Feel its caress. Enjoy the physical embrace of the Spirit through the breeze. Psalm 104:3b–4a says, "You make the clouds Your chariot; You ride upon the wings of the wind. The winds are Your messengers."

You can experience His filling by the release of the mighty wind of the Holy Spirit into your life. Acts 2:2, 4a says, "Suddenly, there was a sound from heaven like the roaring of a mighty windstorm, and it filled the house where they were sitting.... And everyone present was filled with the Holy Spirit." The same Spirit that blew like a mighty wind upon the believers on the day of Pentecost, enabling them to proclaim the gospel in foreign tongues, is the Spirit who will empower you to proclaim the gospel to a generation whose thoughts are foreign to the thoughts of God.

You can set your sail and follow His direction by waiting on the wind of the Holy Spirit. You should be like a sailboat that waits for direction until it catches the wind of God. Go where He leads and the direction His Spirit is blowing.

You can rely on His provision from the winds that bring His blessing. Psalm 78:26–27 tells us: "He released the east wind in the heavens and guided the south wind by His mighty power. He rained down meat as thick as dust—birds as plentiful as the sand on the seashore!"

You can trust in His protection as He displays His mighty power by the fierce winds of His wrath against your enemies. The wind means He is coming to your rescue. Psalm 18:10 says He is coming to deliver: "'Mounted on a mighty angelic being' He flew, soaring on the wings of the wind."

If you know Jesus, you won't fear the wind. It almost makes you want to move to Chicago!

"Serenity is not freedom from the storm but peace amid the storm."
Adrian Rogers

Day 80

The Deception of Self-Protection

The LORD is my strength and shield. I trust Him with all my heart.
Psalm 28:7

Nobody wants to hurt. The irony of self-protection is that the price you pay for it actually costs more than the hurt from which you are supposedly protecting yourself. Self-protection will make you apathetic and cynical. It will make you say things like, "I couldn't care less," or "I'm over it." Of course, you are over it. A self-protected heart has no feeling at all, good or bad.

Statements like that are flashing warning lights on the dashboard of your life. By trying to avoid the pain, you have also killed the joy. You put poison on the weeds and wiped out the flowers.

The God of heaven's armies has provided Himself as a shield of faith for you. Put on the full armor He has provided. His shield will protect you from both poisonous darts and toxic people. Rush to Psalm 91:1–4 which says:

> Those who live in the shelter of the Most High will find rest in the shadow of the Almighty. This I declare about the LORD: He alone is my refuge, my place of safety; He is my God, and I trust Him. For He will rescue you from every trap and protect you from deadly disease. He will cover you with His feathers. He will shelter you with His wings. His faithful promises are your armor and protection.

Can you imagine missing out on some of the most beautiful promises in Scripture? You will miss out if you construct your own walls around your heart. His shield and your walls cannot coexist. It is one or the other. Open up your heart and let your walls down. That's what it means to trust God. Take risks. Forgive. Let Jesus be the One who guards your heart. To "self-protect" is literally to tell the Lord that you are going to do His job because you don't trust Him, need Him, or want Him. Self-protecting is a sin that keeps you from the abundant life. It keeps you from receiving love, and it keeps you from giving love.

"He is not with you in your fortress. He is your fortress."
Adrian Rogers

Day 81

But First, Clean Your Room

If you keep yourself pure, you will be a special utensil for honorable use. Your life will be clean, and you will be ready for the Master to use you for every good work.
2 Timothy 2:21

If you want God to bring new things into your life, some deep cleaning will have to be done first. You can't have both sin and sanctification. Progress is a two-part process. Confession comes before filling. God won't do His work in an unclean vessel any more than you would bake a casserole in a dirty dish. Praise God He is the one who does the cleansing as well! But you must invite Him to do so (see 1 John 1:9).

At our home, I know that if I ever bring anything new into the house, it is going to be a project. My precious husband, Mike, just loves to clean! If any piece of furniture is ever moved an inch, out comes the vacuum cleaner to get what has been hiding underneath it. If anything is added to, or even rearranged on a table or a bookshelf, out comes the dustcloth to prepare the surface for its new inhabitant. He would never put something new in a dirty place. And I am sure that a holy God requires cleanliness far more than a tidy husband!

I will admit that until you begin to clean you don't even notice how dirty things have been. I know from experience that I get used to the dust on the shutters and the woodwork. I hardly notice the cobwebs in the windows and the bugs in the corners. Have you ever looked at what is piled up on top of the ceiling fan blades? Yuck! As you know, I love to sit in my rocker outside and have my quiet time. One day the cold forced me inside, and I looked out the window instead of actually being outside. I didn't even notice the horrible smudges and streaks all over the glass until the sun shone directly on it.

Like the sun through the windowpanes, when the Son shines on your life, you will notice some things you haven't noticed before. And when God begins to rearrange things that are not in the right order, you will find some hidden filth. When God adds new things you have never experienced, you are going to discover a lot of things that need to go in order to make space. You are going to have a lot of exposed areas that need to be cleaned. Satan isn't going to like this process. He hides behind the dust bunnies in your heart.

What are you going to get rid of in your life? There isn't room for both the old and the new. What are you going to clean? God isn't going to redecorate a filthy room.

"The Holy Spirit never leaves a surrendered vessel unfilled or unused."
Adrian Rogers

Day 82

Memorize It, Utilize It, and Weaponize It

Your Word is a lamp to guide my feet and a light for my path.
Psalm 119:105

Oh, how you should long for the Word of God! The psalmist says that in the same way a deer pants for water your heart should long for the Word of God. You should read it. Love it. Claim it. Memorize it. Meditate on it. Obey it. Desire it. Use it. Share it. Cling to it. Trust it. Follow it. But it must get out of your Bible and into your mind. Then, it must get out of your mind and into your heart. And then, it must get out of your heart and into your actions. How do you make this happen?

You must memorize the Scripture. How can you take it with you everywhere you go if it is not inside of you? If you have a hard time memorizing, even the repetitive act of attempting to memorize has utmost value. If you can't seem to get it down word for word, then get it down thought for thought. Try to isolate at least one Scripture a day that you want to claim and attempt to memorize. Type out the Scripture God has laid on your heart for the day and tape it on a four-by-six note card. Carry that note card with you, referring to it throughout the day. This is what I do to make it permanently mine.

You must utilize the Scripture. You have to memorize the Scripture in order to utilize the Scripture. When you interact in the real world, in real time, you won't always have the luxury of an open Bible in front of you. If it is memorized, you will be able to apply it to every conversation. There will be biblical wisdom for every circumstance and biblical instruction for every decision. Your first instinct should be to compare everything you hear throughout the day with the Word of God that is hidden inside of you. As you do this, your thoughts will become His thoughts. You will begin to see life from His perspective. Everything will change.

You must weaponize the Scripture. God's Word defeats the strongholds of Satan. God's Word exposes his lies. God's Word pierces the darkness of the Enemy. God's Word allows you to reclaim captured territory. Even Jesus used the memorized Word of God against Satan. Each day you are admonished to take up the "sword of the Spirit, which is the Word of God" (Eph. 6:17). When you fight with the Word of God, in the power of the Holy Spirit, no enemy can prevail.

"The Bible is God's road map."
Adrian Rogers

Day 83

God Himself Is Your Armor

O LORD, oppose those who oppose me. Fight those who fight against me. Put on Your armor, and take up Your shield. Prepare for battle, and come to my aid. Lift up Your spear and javelin against those who pursue me. Let me hear You say, "I will give you victory!"
Psalm 35:1–3

You don't put on your armor to fight for God. You put on Him. You don't fight for Him. He fights for you. "The battle is the LORD's" (1 Sam. 17:47). The secret is not metal armor, the secret is that the armor is God Himself.

In Ephesians, you are told to "put on the belt of truth" (Eph. 6:14). The question is not: What is the belt of truth? The question is: Who is the belt of truth? Jesus said, "I am the Way, the Truth, and the Life" (John 14:6a). And then put on "the body armor of God's righteousness" (Eph. 6:14). You don't just put on righteousness; you put on God's righteousness. Your righteousness is as "filthy rags" (Isa. 64:6a). "For God made Christ, who never sinned, to be the offering for our sin, so that we could be made right with God through Christ" (2 Cor. 5:21). Your sin cannot be seen because it is covered in the righteousness of Christ. Next, "For shoes, put on the peace that comes from the Good News" (Eph. 6:15a). This good news isn't good news about a job promotion or great checkup from the doctor. This good news is that Jesus lived a sinless life, died a sacrificial death, and was raised a victorious Savior. Ephesians 2:14 says, "For He Himself is our peace" (NKJV).

"In addition to all of these, hold up the shield of faith" (Eph. 6:16a). This isn't faith in faith. It isn't what we believe but whom we believe. Faith is believing that He is who He says He is and that He can do what He says He can do. Psalm 7:10 says, "God is my shield." Then, "Put on salvation as your helmet" (Eph. 6:17). Who is that salvation? "He alone is my rock and my salvation" (Ps. 62:2). He is your salvation.

Finally, "take the sword of the Spirit, which is the Word of God" (Eph. 6:17). John 1:1 tells us who the Word of God is: "In the beginning the Word already existed. The Word was with God, and the Word was God." The armor of God has nothing to do with actual armor. It has nothing to do with you. It is all Him. You put on Him. He fights your battles for you. He will always win.

"Everybody needs a hero. Jesus is mine."
Adrian Rogers

Day 84

Walking in the Fire with Jesus

*We went through fire and flood, but You brought
us to a place of great abundance.*
Psalm 66:12

The beloved passage in Isaiah 43 begins by saying, "Listen to the LORD who created you. O Israel, the One who formed you says, 'Do not be afraid, for I have ransomed you. I have called you by name; you are Mine'" (v. 1). This God who cares even more deeply about your well-being than you could even care about the well-being of your own child says, "When you go through the deep waters, I will be with you. When you go through rivers of difficulty, you will not drown. When you walk through the fire of oppression, you will not be burned up; the flames will not consume you.... You are precious to Me. You are honored, and I love you" (vv. 2, 4b).

God does not say, *If* you go through deep waters, rivers of difficulty, or the fire of oppression. He says, *"When"* you go through them. In John 16:33, Jesus says, "I have told you all this so that you may have peace in Me. Here on earth you will have many trials and sorrows. But take heart, because I have overcome the world."

My parents used to tell me the bedtime story about Shadrach, Meshach, and "To Bed You Go." (I found out later it was Shadrach, Meshach, and Abednego.) These three boys refused to bow down and worship the gold statue made for King Nebuchadnezzar. When commanded to do so, in Daniel 3:17–18, they replied: "If we are thrown in the blazing furnace, the God whom we serve is able to save us. He will rescue us from your power, Your Majesty. But even if He doesn't, we want to make it clear to you, Your Majesty, that we will never serve your gods or worship the gold statue you have set up."

As it turns out, the "even if He does not" clause was activated, and the three boys were thrown into the furnace. But look at this! Daniel 3:24a–25 says, "But suddenly, Nebuchadnezzar jumped up in amazement and exclaimed to his advisories, 'Didn't we tie up three men and throw them into the furnace?' . . . 'Look!' Nebuchadnezzar shouted. 'I see four men, unbound, walking around in the fire unharmed! And the fourth looks like a god!'"

Oh friend, the only thing better than being delivered *from* the fire is being delivered *through* the fire! Can you even fathom being unbound, unharmed, and walking with the literal preincarnate Jesus Christ Himself? He is with you, even now, no matter what fire you are walking through.

"Faith believes in spite of the circumstances
and acts in spite of the consequences."
Adrian Rogers

Day 85

A Little Thing Is a Big Deal

*"If you are faithful in little things,
you will be faithful in large ones."*
Luke 16:10

It is one thing to "rise to the occasion" when you are in front of the microphone and the multitude. It is quite another thing when there is no microphone and there is no multitude. I believe God is most honored when you do the mundane tasks that make up real life in His power and for His glory alone, with no one watching, no one noticing, and definitely no one applauding. God takes delight in you when you do the dishes and take out the trash. He surrounds you with His pleasure when you change the dirty diapers, rock the crying babies, and do another load of laundry.

It is the highest calling of God to do the lowest duties faithfully, day in and day out, for His glory. The premise of the classic book *Practicing the Presence of God* written by Brother Lawrence is that Jesus is just as present when you are doing the dishes in a chaotic kitchen as He is in the solitude of a monastery. He is present in the menial tasks.

Jesus, Himself, lived this sinless life by taking on the "humble position of a slave" (Phil. 2:7). When no one else notices and no one else cares is when God takes notice. The standing ovation of the crowd blocks the vision of God. In obscurity God notices faithfulness most clearly. What are you doing when no one is watching and the task you are performing seems totally unimportant to a world wanting to be impressed by power and position? You can receive your recognition on earth from men, or you can receive your recognition from God. Choose wisely.

Your calling as a homemaker, your calling as an hourly employee, your calling as a humble servant is where the life of Jesus in you shines the brightest. The less noticeable you are, the more noticeable Jesus is. The less you do big things that bring glory and attention to you, the more glory and attention your life is able to bring to God. And if you are faithful in these little things, there may be times when God chooses you to be the one to participate in doing something the world calls big. It is all big to God. But only if you have proven yourself by faithfully doing the mundane in His strength and for His glory will He trust you to do the same in what the world calls mighty and miraculous. You must have the same attitude in both, or even the "big" things you do for God will be burned up at the judgment like wood, hay, and stubble. Thank God for your high calling to be a humble servant. Be prepared for the big moment, but be willing to serve in obscurity. That is where the real heroes are found.

"The big things in life are made up of little acts, little words, little thoughts."
Adrian Rogers

Day 86

God Will Give You More Than You Can Handle

We were crushed and overwhelmed beyond our ability to endure, and we thought we would never live through it. In fact, we expected to die. But as a result, we stopped relying on ourselves and learned to rely only on God, who raises the dead.
2 Corinthians 1:8b–9

I don't even have to ask. I know you have had someone say to you, "It will be okay. God will never give you more than you can handle." That is so wrong, it couldn't be wronger! I know *wronger* isn't a word, but it sure conveys a meaning. On the contrary, God regularly and purposely gives you more than you can handle. He definitely gives you more than you can bear. And He does it intentionally!

God knows that if you could handle it yourself, you would. When you don't pray, when you don't call out to God in desperation, it is the same as saying, "It's okay, Lord. I've got this."

The truth is, you never "have it." Absolutely everything, from your next breath on, is something for which you desperately depend on God, whether you know it or think about it. Your Creator, your Sustainer, is literally your life support. He is the One who gives you your next breath. If you want to experience a terrifying situation, it will be when you have to sit and hold the hand of a loved one who is struggling to take their next breath. I promise that you will cry out to God then.

Right now you may not be struggling for your next breath, but you may be at the end of your rope, at the end of your resources, or at the end of your strength. Take courage. That's where God has put you, and that's where God wants you. You are finally in the position for God to show out and for there to be no question who did it and who gets the glory.

You can be like the apostle Paul and say, "That's why I take pleasure in my weaknesses, and in the insults, hardships, persecutions, and troubles that I suffer for Christ. For when I am weak, then I am strong" (2 Cor. 12:10). Your bad situation is not bad after all. God is setting the stage for a miracle, and you are going to have a front-row seat! Psalm 55:22 promises: "Give your burdens to the LORD, and He will take care of you. He will not permit the godly to slip and fall."

> *"God will put on us more than we can bear but not more than He can bear."*
> **Adrian Rogers**

Day 87

Small but Mighty

He chose things that are powerless.
1 Corinthians 1:27

Please don't ask me why I spent two hours of my precious life watching the movie *Beverly Hills Chihuahua*. I don't think I'll be able to come up with an answer. But I can still remember the Chihuahuas chanting, "We are small but mighty!" It reminds me of Proverbs 30:24–28 which says: "There are four things on earth that are small but unusually wise: Ants—they aren't strong, but they store up food all summer. Hyraxes—they aren't powerful, but they make their homes among the rocks. Locusts—they have no king, but they march in formation. Lizards—they are easy to catch, but they are found even in kings' palaces."

Take heart if you don't feel important or impactful! God delights in using small, insignificant things and definitely unimportant people! God loves to show His power through people who will never be able to take the credit for themselves.

First Corinthians 1:26–31 says,

> Remember, dear brothers and sisters, that few of you were wise in the world's eyes or powerful or wealthy when God called you. Instead, God chose things the world considers foolish in order to shame those who think they are wise. And He chose things that are powerless to shame those who are powerful. God

chose things despised by the world, things counted as nothing at all, and used them to bring to nothing what the world considers important. As a result, no one can ever boast in the presence of God.

All sports seem to revolve around a draft system and a race for who wins the draft lottery and gets to pick first. The future of the franchise depends on picking the most proficient and the most powerful. Even children's sandlot teams are decided by who gets picked first. The potential of the team is in the hands of the person who makes the player selections just as much, or more, as in the hands of the players themselves.

When God announces His picks, He chooses in reverse order. The first ones He selects aren't big, strong, or fast. While man selects the giant, Goliath, God scouts the sheepfold and selects the shepherd boy, David. Your smallness is the exact place He longs to occupy. Little is much when God is in it!

"What we need is not great faith but faith in a great God."
Adrian Rogers

Day 88

The Lost Art of the Handwritten Note

Here is my greeting in my own handwriting—Paul. I do this in all my letters to prove they are from me.
2 Thessalonians 3:17

If there is something of spiritual significance that you want someone to save for years to come, you need to write a handwritten note. Yes, typing is so much quicker. Certainly, texting is instant. Emailing is far easier. But people don't delete a handwritten letter. A letter takes time and thought. Most letters are kept, cherished, and reread for years to come. Everywhere I go I see letters that are years old but are still pinned onto bulletin boards in people's offices. Do you have a supply of note cards and greeting cards on hand? Do you have postage stamps on hand? Do you know personal addresses? How many will you commit to write? Just one note a day is thirty a month.

When you are praying for someone, put it into writing. Even if your loved one's heart is not open when they initially receive your letter, hearts can change over time. They can reread it when they are ripe. You are responsible for obedience and action. God is responsible for acceptance and timing.

I have a dear friend who writes her prayers out and sends them to another dear friend. Most people just say, "I am praying for you." This friend writes out her prayers. This goes a step further. The friend she is praying for then copies those prayers and sends them out to her friends, requesting that they join in by praying the same prayer. The impact is tenfold. I didn't like multiplication in school, but I love it in life!

Handwritten letters can be passed from generation to generation. They can keep a faith history alive in a family. Joel 1:3 says, "Tell your children about it in the years to come, and let your children tell their children. Pass the story down from generation to generation." You have to write it down to pass it down. Your loved ones can know your desires for them long after you are gone by your handwritten notes. God can use your letters to convict a wayward child long after your death. This is a way you can say the same thing over and over again. Try it!

> *I've seen hundreds of personal letters signed by my father that ended with "God is love. Jesus is wonderful."*
> **Adrian Rogers**

Day 89

Are You Emotionally Needy?

*Give all your worries and needs to God,
for He cares for you.*
1 Peter 5:7

Emotional neediness reveals a lot about you. But one thing it shows for sure is that Christ is not everything to you. There is nothing wrong with having a "heart hunger," but when that emptiness is filled with anyone other than Christ, it is idolatry. When you run to another human being to soothe your neediness, you are allowing the empty spaces God desires to fill with Himself to be filled with the other person. When you feel hurt by another person, it is an indicator that you have cracks that are not filled with God. You have allowed someone else to penetrate those cracks and take over the controls of your emotions.

I know this raises several real questions. Even if you are allowing Christ to fill you completely, won't there still be times of legitimate ache and hurt? The answer is yes. In times of loss and hurt, you will experience the same emotions as everyone else, but it will not affect you the same way. You will be able to maintain an unshakable faith and a deep inner joy, no matter what happens. You will not fall apart or go to pieces. You will be affected, but you will be able to "give all your worries and cares to God, for He cares about you" (1 Pet. 5:7).

You might also think that not needing anyone but God sounds like a self-centered approach to life. It almost sounds as if you are an island that needs no one and who feels no pain. It is confusing because God commands you to relate to one another. You are commanded to give, expecting nothing in return. What you must realize is that until your relationship with Christ is everything, you will have nothing to give or offer to anyone else. The only way you can love others with a selfless love is to love with the love of Christ. You must be filled to the point of overflowing in order to love with an agape love.

If you have to have someone to complete you, you will be using them instead of loving them. You will be trying to get from them when you should be giving to them. Needing no one else besides Christ will actually make you into the most relational person alive. You will see everyone through Christ's eyes and love them with Christ's love. It will permeate your entire being and ooze out of your pores. It's a new way to live.

"God is searching our hearts in order to supply our deepest need."
Adrian Rogers

Day 90

Let God Work the Night Shift

It is useless for you to work so hard from early morning until late at night, anxiously working for food to eat; for God gives rest to His loved ones.
Psalm 127:2

Have you ever felt like too many activities and responsibilities have piled up in your life and have caused a traffic jam? When that happens to me, it affects my attitude and my demeanor. I get touchy and snappy. Have you been there? When I am there, I realize it is time to check the fuel tank. When I work overtime, it is almost always me trying to make things happen on my own, in my own strength, and in my own power. Many times when I am a self-proclaimed workaholic, I proclaim it as something for which I should be proud. It isn't. A workaholic is someone who is living her life by the motto: "Me! Me! Me! It all depends on me!" If you feel that way, there is a big red flashing light on the dashboard that says, "Warning: you are operating in the flesh. You are running on fumes. You must stop and fill up with Jesus."

I was wide-awake at 5:00 a.m. thinking about what needed to be done, after working until midnight the night before. I had been edgy and irritable with Mike before dinner and just generally out of sorts. My mind went to one of my favorite verses, Psalm 127:2. I love the interpretation of this verse from the Amplified Bible:

> It is vain for you to rise early,
> To retire late,

To eat the bread of anxious labors—
For He gives [blessings] to His beloved even in his
   sleep.

No one, including me and including you, can work without "margin" in their life and experience the joy of the Lord. You don't need to put in sixteen-hour days to get it all done. You do need to work, but you don't need to overwork. Put in a strong eight hours of work, followed by another eight hours to rest, refresh, reset, recreate, and relate to those you love. Then sleep the final eight hours. Regardless of what you feel you need to do, you can sleep peacefully because you know God is working the night shift. He is giving "to His beloved even in his sleep." The good things that happen in your life don't depend on you. God is the great multiplier, and He goes to work when you close your eyes and rest in His provision. I know that the best things that have happened for me have been things that I didn't have my fingerprints on. They were things that happened "while I was sleeping."

> *"Go to bed tonight and sleep well. Rest your head on your pillow and pillow your soul on the promises of God, for the God who watches over Israel neither slumbers nor sleeps."*
> **Adrian Rogers**

Notes

1. Bob Beaudine, *2 Chairs: The Secret That Changes Everything* (Brentwood, TN: Worthy Books, August 2016).

2. Sarah Ban Breathnach quote from https://www.goodreads.com/author/quotes/3495853.Sarah_Ban_Breathnach.

3. John Stick, *Follow the Cloud* (Colorado Springs, CO: Multnomah, 2017), 191.

4. Martin Luther, AZQuotes.com, accessed June 15, 2024, https://www.azquotes.com/quote/353476.

5. https://www.zameen.com/blog/building-foundation-importance.html and https://advice.pk/blogs/foundation-in-building.php.

6. Eric Thomas quote, https://quotefancy.com/quote/1578929/Eric-Thomas-Fall-in-love-with-the-process-and-the-results-will-come

7. Frederick Lehman, "The Love of God" (1917). Public domain.

8. Charles Stanley quote found in Frances Thompson, *The Hound of Heaven* (New York: McCracken Press, 1993).

9. Sir Winston Churchill quote, https://www.goodreads.com/quotes/49610-before-you-can-inspire-with-emotion-you-must-be-swamped

10. Elisa Henry, "John C. Maxwell: Looking Upward," Success, August 27, 2013, https://www.success.com/john-c-maxwell-looking-upward.

11. Kenneth Blanchard, *The One Minute Manager* (New York: William Morrow, 2015).

12. William J. Gaither, "He Touched Me" (1963).

13. Robert Robinson, "Come Thou Fount" (1758). Public domain.

Personal Reflection

Personal Reflection

Personal Reflection

Personal Reflection

Personal Reflection

DEVOTIONALS ALSO AVAILABLE
FROM B&H PUBLISHING

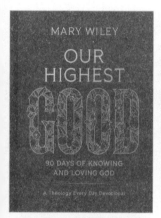

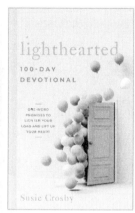

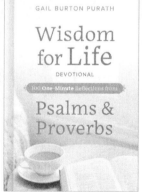
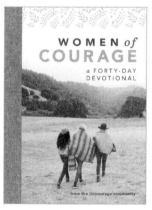